Space/Time Magic

Taylor Ellwood

IMMANION PRESS
Stafford, England

Space/Time Magic
By Taylor Ellwood
© 2005

http://taylorellwood.chaosmagic.com/

Cover: Todd Heilmann
Art Direction and Typesetting: Gabriel Strange
Editor: Donald Hardy

Set in Times

First edition by Immanion Press, 2005

0 9 8 7 6 5 4 3 2 1

An Immanion Press Edition
http://www.immanionpress.wox.org
info@immanionpress.wox.org

ISBN 1-9048-5326-9

Space/Time Magic

Reviews of Pop Culture Magick by Taylor Ellwood

Pop Culture Magick Reviewed in Pagan Muse, 5 out of 5 stars!

Being of the generation X grouping, I found Taylor Ellwood's Pop Culture Magick to be highly thematic for the times. I can't be the only one who sees the necessity of the subject, nor the obvious validity of the magickal path he describes. I have children who watch Anime, I play an RPG with magickal connotations; from where do folks suppose the mythos and magick for those current cultural icons come from? It didn't just appear on its own.

Uh huh, I thought so - your brain is working now, isn't it?

Taylor has, in a quiet way, forced minds to work. I have to wonder how many "Ah HA!"s sounded across campuses and in homes after the book was released. Even though I had made those cross-references in playing the games and watching the Anime with the kids, I caught myself saying "Of course!" and "How could I have missed that before?".

Even Bugs Bunny is not immune to observation and scrutiny - and finding the archetype within the cell.

Taylor has found the bridge between generations and explained the path in such a way that no one should be able to walk away from the book confused. Just watch an episode of Pokemon, you'll see it.

by Ierne Editor - Pagan Muse

Review of Pop Culture Magick by Vaughan of Pagannews

I've said it before and I'll say it again. You can use Pokemon characters as points of focus for ritual if you really want. Taylor Ellwood's new book Pop Culture Magick explores this concept in a lot more depth., examining ways that we can use contemporary icons in place of deities from ancient times. Undoubtedly, some people will be offended by this concept. For that reason, I think that this book would be most beneficial for those people that are quite far along in their personal spiritual path, and have come to realize that the public images of Britney Spears, Buffy the Vampire Slayer and Captain Kirk are clearly egregors; Constructs worshipped on a daily basis and on a much larger scale than Isis or Dagda or Thor (unless you're talking about the Thor from Marvel Comics). In this books the author forces us to face the truth of that, and it is a truth that many people may not be ready or willing to accept.

It is clear that the author has studied a lot of the different genres in detail, because there are an incredible number of references from Advanced Dungeons & Dragons to Star Trek. For those readers that can get past the obvious paradox of not wanting to accept pop culture idols as actual idols, Ellwood includes several useful pathworking exercises, suggestions for franchies to use as a base pantheon (Star Wars, Dragonball Z etc) and also shows us how to set up a Pop Culture Altar. The meat of the book is in the first 161 pages, followed by the seven appendices that provide a lot of useful reference information. It is a relatively quick read, although it will take longer if you pause to do the exercises at the end f each chapter. All in all, I enjoyed this book. I don't think I am ready to set up an altar to Arthur Dent in the hope that he can provide me with the Question to the Answer of Life, The Universe and Everything (the answer being `42'). But the book has certainly given me food for thought and discussion. In the final analysis, that is really what matters...

Pop Culture Magick by Taylor Ellwood Review by Gwinevere Rain

If you read the last issue of Copper Moon E-zine you may have come across a unique article that involved a melding of Harry Potter and real magick. Who would come up with such a different concept? Two words - Taylor Ellwood. He is the author of Pop Culture Magick. In this book we see an analysis of contemporary culture icons with magick intertwined.

The underlying theory isn't bubblegum witchcraft but instead more occult philosophy. On page 51 the author writes, "When you or I believe in a concept, we give it reality and when a lot of people believe in it, they give it power."

Topics range from TV characters, Sci-fi shows, cartoons, comics and video games. It is important to note that this isn't directly a Wicca book. Where as some practitioners may be interested in utilizing this eclectic format its overall theme is an occult based system of magick.

Most notable is Ellwood's authentic passion for this subject. I applaud his creativity and willingness to challenge traditional views.

Also by Taylor Ellwood

Creating Magickal Entities
(with David Michael Cunningham and Amanda R. Wagner)

Pop Culture Magick
(also available through Immanion Press)

Dedication

I dedicate this book to my father, for showing me a person can change no matter what his age, to Lee and Maegdlyn for looking out for me, and to Maryam for trusting me.

To Jennifer

In Identity Midoniverse

Taylor

G Greed

Acknowledgments

I'd like to acknowledge all the people who have helped me put this book together. Storm, Gabby and Lydia at Immanion Press have been invaluable in giving this book the once over to make sure it's in your hands now. Donald Hardy, my patient copy-editor, waded bravely through my writing so that it was easier to read. John Coughlin was kind enough to write the introduction of this book and I am very thankful to him for that, as well as the kind words he wrote. Read his books and I think you'll find a lot of insight in what he has to offer. Rose Wakely, I appreciate your stalwart friendship. Todd, for coming up with another brilliant cover and being a good friend. The time machines e-list I ran has also been very helpful in experimenting with my approaches and offering valuable feedback. The Paleonova e-list has also been invaluable in promoting me. Also to those of you like Maegdlyn, Lee, Steven, Lupa, The Tribe of the Triple Phoenix, D. J. Lawrence and Alex (Peristera) who have looked out for me and gotten me into events, I appreciate your help and dedication to my ideas. Finally to Maryam, for trusting me and showing me how a relationship can change and bring with it many new possibilities.

Table of Contents

Foreword

In this book I've chosen to use the word "magic," instead of "magick." I've noticed that a lot of my fellow writers do this, and I also have noticed that I've habitually used magick without really thinking about it. I think it's always important to think about the words you use, because those words carry with them many meanings and histories. As with my other writing, you'll find some intriguing book references in here. I urge you to look into those citations and try out some of the ideas expressed in those books as a complement to this book. Also within this book, I've tried to show not only completed projects, but also works in process. I don't believe that any technique is ever finished, but I also think it's important to show the process of how a technique comes to be refined through experimentation. APA style has been used for the citations in this text and for the bibliography.

The internal citation style has been changed by the publisher to conform to a UK standard used by them.

Introduction

We stand at the threshold of a new generation of magic, rooted not in the formal setting of old school ritual magic, a la the great lodges, but fed by the first generation of popular chaotes such as Carroll and Hine. The seeds that those pioneers planted are now blooming through the works of authors such as Taylor Ellwood.

Times have changed, and the world of the modern day magician is very different from that of the forefathers of traditional western ritual magic. Like every generation, we seek new models and new vocabulary to bridge the gap between this ideal of magic with our ever-developing grasp of reality. Perhaps one hundred years from now new generations will smirk at these new models, just as we smirk at some of the antiquated ideas of earlier magicians.

The problem that most face with models is that we tend to take them so damn seriously. A model is not the final answer – it is a stepping stone. A model is not the reality, but a representation of a *perceived* reality. It serves a purpose, but has its limitations.

Consider the Bohr's model of the atom we learned in high school chemistry (they still teach that, right?). Before the advent of wave theories and modern quantum mechanics, it seemed to have all the answers, and was a huge step above the classical models, opening the door to a whole new level of science. However, once our scope began to go beyond the atomic level into the subatomic, that model, as well as our perception of the makeup of physical reality, began to unravel. Yet the model still has practical applications, so long as you use it within the scope of its limitations.

Our perception of reality itself is but a model, based on our subjective experiences of it (and what we have been told). We think we have all the answers, until some odd synchronicity makes us wonder just what is really happening "out there" beyond the scope of our very limited physical senses. It would seem the reality we know is not as solid as we like to think.

What is low magic but the attempt to understand those unknown forces that influence the objective universe so that we can harness them to our benefit? The distinction between the subjective universe (how we perceive it) and the objective universe (that which is independent of our perceptions) is a fuzzy one at best. Both in science and in magic each appears to influence the other. The observer and the observed interact in some unknown cosmic dance that transcends mere time and space.

Probably the most frightening thing about magic, which every magician ultimately must face, is that it really does work and we haven't a clue why. Oh, we have our theories – our models – but they are only useful until an exception is found, at which point our models either expand and adapt, or we try to explain the exception away, lest our models crumble before our eyes. We experiment and observe, and glimpses of these unknown mechanics are expressed through occult symbolism and jargon. But sometimes we trade one self-limiting model for another. Does it really matter, for instance, if I do a love spell on a certain hour of a certain day during a certain phase of the moon? For some it does. Their models do not adapt, and they work only so long as one does not ask too many questions.

A magician must not only question reality, but also question his or her own perceptions of it. Our beliefs are more conditioning than we may care to accept. Much of what we believe to be "true" rests purely on the fact that we were told so. Our perceptions reflect the biases of the society and culture in which we were raised. This becomes more apparent when we begin to look at other cultures. Consider gender roles; in some countries it is not uncommon to see men weep openly at funerals. Being raised in a society where men are discouraged to show such "weakness," despite knowing on an intellectual level that such expressions of emotion are psychologically healthy, chances are most of the male readers here go out of their way to hide their tears.

Consider also how little we know of the effects our own unconscious influences. We like to think of ourselves as being composed of an individual Self, yet as we meditate we find contradictory thoughts and feelings welling up from the depths of the mind. Many of the voices in our heads seem to have a life of their own. Those who have explored the realm of individuation and shadow work of Jungian psychology know only too well how insidious projection can be in influencing our perceptions. We project the worst of our own nature onto the sins of others. We project the blame for our failings on a cruel Universe out to get us. Those who dare walk a magical path don't have the luxury of such scapegoats, for they have the audacity to claim ownership of their lives and seek to change both themselves and the Universe to their liking.

While the ideas within this treatise alone will provide much food for thought, the true gems are the exercises found at the end of each chapter. This is where you apply these ideas to your own life, to your own subjective reality. This is where the magic will be found!

Magic is ultimately about doing. Memorizing Enochian keys or collecting the most rare and expensive paraphernalia might impress the ignorant, but what do you have to show for them? Sure, they may be useful tools, but they are not the magic. That is an internal alchemy that rests solely within the magician, and not the props and affiliations we adorn ourselves with.

The magician has the desire to ask "what if?" and the guts to then go and find out. Read these ideas and you might learn something new; play with these ideas and you will grow. That is the way of the magician. To truly glimpse these mysteries one must experience them first hand, not read about them in a book. I stress this point *ad nauseum*, having wasted more years than I care to share before I learned this lesson.

Interestingly enough (as synchronicities often are), just prior to being invited to write this introduction I was pondering my own space-time magical perceptions. Whenever I find myself in a new and different place I wonder what I would have been like had I grown up there. How much of who I am would have been the same with those different childhood experiences? Consider merely the delicate web of events that brought the words you are reading now to manifest. Being what one may call an "obscure occult author," I don't make a habit of promoting my work, assuming that those who would best benefit from it will eventually stumble across it when the time is right. It was thus a surprise to me when I was invited to speak at Winterstar 21, and pure chance that I actually decided to accept it. Had I not attended, I would not have had the pleasure of meeting the author of this book, or, for that matter, had I not read and been intrigued by his article *Invoking Buffy*, I might not have been inclined to conversation, especially given my tendency to not be very talkative. The more I examine the factors which led me to this point, the more *im*probable it seems, yet here you are reading these very words, flowing from inspiration after having read a draft of this very book. And who knows? Chances are now that you have read these words perhaps you will start to stumble across my name more... as if perhaps, just perhaps, this brief encounter with my writing has somehow influenced you toward such probabilities... hmmm.... could this introduction in its own right be a magical working of space/time?

The other magical perception, which I had been pondering, was again a synchronistic encounter. While randomly surfing the Internet instead of doing my work, I came across an interesting essay on magic and probabilities. The general gist of the essay was that the future always consists of many potential outcomes, some more probable than others, given the current environmental factors in play. If I were to somehow tap into a specific probable outcome, perhaps I could "follow" that specific path or current, and thus reach a future closer to that desired outcome than otherwise... something akin to hooking a fish and reeling it in.

Like any magical theory, it sounded great on paper, but it's the experimentation that is essential. So, being in an optimistic and slightly devious mood, I decided, why not play the lottery over the next few weeks, both before and during the experiment. The experiment itself was simple. During a meditative state, I visualized the various futures as spheres, which cluster around spheres of similar outcomes. I then attempted to "resonate" with the spheres associated with winning the jackpot. Each sphere had a different "feeling," and as I identified with a given sphere that feeling internalized within me, and I felt that potential reality as certainty. And now I am a millionaire...ok, maybe not a "millionaire," but I did win SOMETHING more often after my meditations (granted I only won $1 to $3 when I won at all). It was subtle, but there did seem to be a slight influence in my favor. When all was said and done, I may not have walked away with a new house, but I did buy myself a nice cup of tea and a donut from the resulting profit of this working. From a magician's point of view that's pretty damn good, given the odds of winning, and the little I could do to improve my odds apart from buying the tickets and doing the meditations.

So these peculiar thoughts and experiences were fresh in my mind, when out of the blue Taylor invited me to write this introduction, giving me an opportunity to read his thoughts and experiences with space/time magic long before the book would be published, and at a time I would most appreciate the material. Again the Universe seemed to respond to my need, a synchronicity not uncommon among practicing magicians.

Apart from the various exercises in this book, there is one area I would like to emphasize, since it is probably one of the least appreciated areas of magical training: awareness exercises. Regardie and the Ciceros present some great exercises within their Golden Dawn materials so I'll quickly share my variations of their work here.

External Awareness

Every day, while walking to work, or while wandering the mall, spend at least 15 minutes observing the details of all your senses. What do you smell? What do you hear? What do you see? How does the ground feel? Note how you can usually feel certain textures, even with your shoes on. I suggest concentrating on one sense each day at first, so as not to be overloaded.

Internal Awareness

Every day, while meditating or sitting in a train (or somewhere you will not be disturbed), close your eyes, relax, and spend 15 minutes becoming aware of what is happening to your body. The more relaxed you are the better for this, so start out with a relaxation exercise of some sort. Feel the seat pressing back against you, feel the air flow in and out as you breathe, feel your heart beat and how the pulse can actually be felt in certain areas of your body and even make a slight sound against your clothing. Feel the various discomforts that tend to pop up as distractions.

Once you have had some practice with this, start to note also the thoughts and feelings which seem to well out of nowhere in reaction to your otherwise growing inner silence. Become aware of how your body reacts to them. Try to remain a passive observer, not lingering on these sensations and thoughts, but merely observing and acknowledging.

I know...BORING! But they can also be fun when approached as play. It takes time to realize the progress, but the eventual benefits are worth it. By improving our awareness we eventually become aware of just how *un*aware we really are. We spend much of our day like wind-up robots, reacting partly by instinct and partly by conditioning to various stimuli. Think about how you get to work or school. I successfully navigate through New York City rush hour on foot every day, and yet on most days could not tell you how I got from point A to point B. I am on autopilot, consciousness only kicking in when something unexpected suddenly crossed my path, such as a taxi running a red light or a lost tourist not knowing how to walk in a straight line. Fact is, we spend more time in this daze than we realize, and end up stuck living in the same patterns, which seem to plague our lives.

A sorcerer seeks to break those patterns by acting consciously and maintaining a greater degree of awareness. Through that process one begins to peel away the conditioning that filters our perceptions. Reality becomes less what we are told it is and more what we experience it as... seems so simple in writing, yet it is a lifelong path of enlightenment.

While magic may be perceived as a means to opening new doors, I would argue that underlying that is the means of *discovering* new doors. The practice of magic makes us aware of a universe full of subtle influences and causalities. We become aware not only of the impact of these influences on us, but of our impact on them...and on ourselves. I often use the Jungian model of psychology to discover the various ways in which we create our own limitations and dilemmas. But like every model, it has its limitations, despite its practical applications. This book uses a model of nonlinear time to show the same principle. If we are victims, it is very often to our own folly...whether we choose to realize it or not.

Perhaps this is one of the reasons why magic is said to potentially drive one insane. Any self-reflective system would share that dubious honor, but magic more so because it provides enough room for self-delusion. It's hard not to come across cases of people lost in delusions of grandeur, and while this might be entertaining, it should serve as a reality check. More so, magic forces us to realize we are at the driver's seat of our lives, and that we often leave it on autopilot.

I'll end this ramble of an introduction with one more observation. While attending a few Pagan workshops recently, I noticed an interesting keyword being used over and over again...*manifest*. I am not sure if this was a local adoption, or a new trendy phrase within the magical community, but either way it is a great word. From the point of view of space/time, our experiences manifest from our interactions with the world, and we manifest ourselves from those experiences. The magician can realize this process and become aware of the fact that at every moment we are *re*manifesting ourselves. I am not the same person I was yesterday. When my life is uneventful, I might remain a similar person to the one I was a moment ago, but occasionally we have an experience that forces us to rethink everything. Call it what you may...a paradigm shift, a dark night of the soul, an initiatory experience...this experience shatters current perceptions of ourselves and the Universe, and all that has since come to pass is seen in a different light. We remanifest ourselves within that new context and are changed forever. To me, this is the path of the magician: to constantly remanifest oneself by expanding one's perceptions of reality and ourselves...to continuously transcend perceived limitations and take one step closer to manifesting our true potential. It's the maintaining of true consciousness, as opposed to the reliance on the autopilot we mistake for it. The magician carves his or her own way through the Universe, and does not merely flow with the current through preexisting channels. As such, magic is not the path for the masses, no matter how trendy it becomes in the mainstream. Most prefer to be led and seek the comfortable numbness of autopilot. Magicians are the troublemakers. We ask too many questions; we recognize and challenge the models we have been conditioned to perceive as reality.

Yes, my friends, magic truly is dangerous! It awakens sleeping minds and returns power to the individual. For this we shall ever remain an outcast lot!

John J. Coughlin
New York
September 2004

Bibliography

Cicero, Chic & Sandra Tabatha, Self-initiation Into The Golden Dawn Tradition. St. Paul: *Llewellyn Publications.* *(1995)*

Regardie, Israel, The One Year Manual. York Beach: *Samuel Weiser Books.* *(1981)*

Chapter One:
What is Space/Time Magic?

I first developed an interest in space/time magic through one of the unlikeliest of mediums: Miss Cleo. A friend and I had decided to make Miss Cleo into a goddess-form of divination. We figured that the amount of energy directed toward her by the media made her into a funnel of power. We wanted to access that power and improve our own divinatory abilities. We weren't concerned with whether or not she was a fake. Evidently some people believed in her, or at least gave her energy, and that energy could be used to improve our skills. When I did my meditation to Miss Cleo, she showed me more than just how to improve my divinatory skills. She revealed to me a multiverse pregnant with probabilities, and showed me that, with awareness of those probabilities, I could manifest reality to my will, or at least do so more successfully than I had before. She showed me that divination was just the tip of the iceberg of what space/time magic could do for me.

Space/time has always fascinated me, particularly with how science has attempted to explain how it works, and how magic has, in turn, attempted to manipulate space/time with the express purpose of helping a person to manifest a particular reality. With space/time, what we are really dealing with is not just space or time, but also reality and our understanding of reality. Space and time are just two dimensions of reality, with many other dimensions being worked with as well. For the purposes of this book, when I refer to space/time magic I'm referring to magic that alters reality, that changes what we consider reality to be.

What that means is that reality is more malleable than most perceive it to be. It also means that working space/time magic isn't necessarily about time travel, but is more about being aware of the probabilities in your life, and how best to make them become reality. Of course, because this book is about space/time, it does include some work with time. We may not be able physically to travel through time, but magic does grant us a means to shift our perspective, to get past the limited linear model of time that most people believe exists. We are not limited to a single line of time, an inevitable march of reality. Instead, we have multiple probabilities, multiple realities, and part of space/time magic is learning to navigate those probabilities through a different understanding of what time is and how it can be worked with once we free our perception from linear reality.

Most chaos magicians are familiar with Peter Carroll's blending of science, math, and magic, particularly when it comes to space/time magic. For this book, while I will draw on the sciences and even mathematical magical approaches to space/time magic, my goal is to present a variety of different angles – or perspectives, if you will – on space/time magic that I don't believe are normally considered by the majority of magicians who practice it. Or if the angle is considered, it's treated with disdain, in a manner that suggests that the perspective should be dropped, as opposed to explored.

Each of the approaches in this book is a radical exploration of how to work with space/time to shape reality. The best way to approach all of this is with an open mind and a desire to come up with your own approaches toward working with space/time magic. All I can offer you are models that have worked for me and continue to work for me. But a creative magician can easily extend my work into different directions I have not imagined, and that is one of the goals of this book. To help you achieve that, at the end of each chapter you will find exercises designed to get you to work with the ideas presented in the chapter.

Before we get to those exercises, however, let's consider how most people view space/time today. Generally, when the majority of people think of it at all, they think the following: "Time and space were a background in which events took place, but which weren't affected by them. Time was separate from space and was considered to be a single line, or a railroad track that was infinite in both directions" (The Universe in a Nutshell - 2001, *Stephen Hawking*, p 32). This is a Newtonian science explanation of space/time. Although contemporary science has disproved this model, many people still live and believe in it. Usually, this model of space/time is referred to as linear. When we think of linear time, for instance, we think of it as a series of events that occur one after the other. The best analogy to use is that of a technical manual, where you have progressive steps. Step one leads to step two and from there step three. This model of time, while seemingly infinite, runs only in one direction, so that once an event occurs, nothing can seemingly be done to change it. And though it would seem that space/time is just part of the background in this model, nonetheless nothing can be done to change it. With linear time, we are stuck in a static reality, with little if any awareness of probability.

And this lack of awareness, this lack of perception, is a large problem when it comes to space/time magic. If we are caught in this paradigm of one event happening after another, then we are stuck with the idea that there is only one past, one present, and one future. We lose perception and seek a comfortable numbness in this paradigm. Or rather, the majority of humanity does, while the minority, including magicians, seeks to expand their horizons beyond the limits of linear reality.

But why do people choose linear reality? Linear reality, being so static, would seemingly be a choice you'd avoid, but many people prefer to avoid responsibility and awareness. Instead, they allow themselves to be trapped in a single line, when in fact there is a third, fourth, and fifth dimension (if not more) that we can use to navigate ourselves to the best probabilities we seek to manifest into our lives. I think that what it comes down to is sanity. The sanity of the average person is far more comfortable with a linear model of reality, one that allows him or her to fit into whatever niche or hole s/he has been told to go to.

However, there are other approaches to space/time that a magician can use that are far more flexible than the linear model in which so many people are trapped. The key is to be aware of how to build your own model of what space/time – of what reality – is. And it is also important to be aware of the other factors that affect reality that we must work with. Einstein's general theory of relativity, for instance, shows that space/time is curved or warped by gravity. This warping affects space/time, specifically the possibilities of space/time, in that it allows that space/time to become dynamic and essential to how the multiverse works and operates, instead of just being the background. Hawking best explains what this theory is:

> General relativity combines the time dimension with the three dimensions of space to form what is called spacetime. The theory incorporates the effects of gravity by saying that the distribution of matter and energy in the universe warps and distorts spacetime, so that it is not flat. Objects in this spacetime try to move in straight lines, but because spacetime is curved, their paths appear bent. They move as if affected by a gravitational field.
> (The Universe in a Nutshell - 2001, *Stephen Hawking*, p. 35)

On the surface, this theory seems to describe a purely physical phenomenon, but in fact it can also operate beyond what is physical, affecting even how we understand and work with space/time in magical ways.

Consider, for instance, that many magicians believe in other planes or universes of existence. Obviously, these universes don't exist in our universe, but to access them we manipulate space/time, and though we may not physically go to these other planes of existence (as far as we know), we nonetheless interact with them, because of the warping of space/time. But if everything was flat and in a straight line, we'd never know of the existence of other planes of existence, because we could not perceive them in any shape or form. Now, the general theory of relativity is supplemented by quantum theories of gravity, which can explain the uncertainty principles that create, in my mind, the probabilities that exist for all of us. But then again, can these theories explain everything?

Even if the theories can help generate some understanding, ultimately it is how you, as magic practitioners, choose to understand space/time that will allow you to manifest your probabilities into reality. Science is one paradigm that explains what space/time is, but there are other paradigms, and they are just as useful in understanding and manipulating space/time. For a magician, any paradigm is just a tool to be used, and with that idea in mind, my purpose for this book is to introduce you to a number of techniques and paradigms that I have successfully used in my own space/time workings. Science is one paradigm I have used and I'll go into that in a later chapter, but what I've noticed in the magical workings that concern space/time is too much of an emphasis on a synthesis of only science and magic. There are other ways of working with space/time beyond this synthesis.

From Phil Hine's perspective, we can understand time in the following sense:

> Although we experience Time as a separate dimension, it is in actuality a byproduct of Consciousness. We are constantly moving backwards and forwards in terms of experienced Past (memory) and anticipated Futures (fantasy). Although much of magical practice is concerned with the ability to remain in the immediate present, it is also useful to be able to make use of our personal Past and Futures.
> (Condensed Chaos - 1995, *Phil Hine,* p. 63)

I agree with Hine's definition of time, though I would change past to pasts. Sometimes the memories you have of the past are not accurate memories to this specific life, but there is always the possibility that memories of the past that aren't accurate can be past memories of other versions of you, or if past lives are something you believe in, memories from a past life. Regardless of that, the past is not limited to a single line, but can branch out with possibilities, just as the future does. Still, even this

31

definition is just another paradigm of what space/time is. There are more paradigms we can use.

To give you a few brief examples, I like to use comics, DNA, words, collages, sigils, and technology to work space/time magic. I also incorporate science and some of the more traditional magical approaches to my work. But all a magician really requires is the will, the imagination, and the desire to understand not merely what space/time is, but how the rules can be bent, or even broken.

However, it is important to first understand what space/time is. I've already told you of the linear reality in which most people live. The rest of this book will focus on the nonlinear reality that, in my opinion, truly exists. I want to present a paradigm of it, *my* paradigm to be exact. You don't need to agree with how I understand space/time…after all, this is just a model I'm using for my convenience. But I choose to use it to provide you with a framework and methodology on which you can build your own paradigm of space/time.

Space/time is a very non-linear experience. To my mind, there is not one straight line that depicts everything that has happened or will happen. Rather, there are multiple pasts, presents, and futures. And all of these multiple pasts, presents, and futures present probabilities for us that we might never consider if we aren't aware they exist. In one sense, non-linear space/time is like a tree. A tree can't exist on one root. Instead, it spreads a network of roots outward, and does likewise with its branches. So, too, you cannot exist on just one probability. Indeed, you would not even have the ability to make a choice if you only had one probability.

Space/time magic is about finding the choices and opportunities, and making the most of those opportunities. Sometimes this involves strategy and finding ten solutions to one problem, and sometimes it involves an awareness of the circumstances that affect you and learning to bend to those circumstances, so that in time you can bend them to your will. Space/time is also a DNA spiral of planets and stars going down, up, and parallel to our reality, representing all the versions of you and I that could be. You can travel to any of those versions, learn from them, and even become them, because they are part and parcel of you.

I also perceive space/time as a realm of shifting probabilities. When one change is made, some probabilities cease to exist, while others come into existence. This is mirrored within our lives. We each make choices and they affect the choices we have made, make, and will make, but even in making those choices, we still have a means to revisit the probabilities that existed before.

Let us consider the role of synchronicity. Often, in our lives, we have events occur that, on the surface, have no relationship with each other, but when examined in a different perspective we find that the events actually do relate to each other. This is called synchronicity. I see synchronicity as a form of space/time magic. As a personal example of this, I had a couple of situations occur in my life and other people's lives that drew us together, despite the physical distance between us. I had two acquaintances, who became friends of mine (Fenwick Rysen and Xi O'Teaz), and who were very interested in experimenting with magic and in the idea of forming a teaching school. Fenwick, in particular, is focused on defining a terminology of magic that can be used to bridge the gaps in discourse within high level magic practice. Xi and I have both been offering him critiques and ideas on his current work. At the same time that he started his work, I was also beginning my own work on the literacy of magic, a concept that had interested me for a while. This concept was somewhat similar to what Fenwick is working on, and so this synchronicity of starting work on similar magic projects gave Xi and us a chance to bounce ideas off each other, and also to get started on building the foundations of a school for magic practice. And since my initial discussions with them, I have also met other people interested in examining the terminology of magic and its place in community. I've often noted that people who are inclined to experiment with magic tend to work on similar ideas and concepts as other experimenters, even if they don't know their fellow experimenters. On the surface, none of these events is overtly related to the other, except that there is a message for me in the events. I learned from situations like the one I mentioned above – where two or more people are working on similar ideas and may not even know that they are – that particular patterns of discourse emerge in the consciousness of people at the same time, so that those people can work together. The synchronicity creates the probability of working together, once experimenters learn that others are working on similar topics. In the case of the event mentioned above, Fenwick and I had interests that occurred synchronously to each other, and were synchronicities, giving me the message that I could not only work with and share information with Fenwick and Xi O'Teaz, but that I could also find a community of like minded people who wanted to experiment and explore the limits of magic. Synchronicity, though not a direct form of magic, is still nonetheless a potent space/time magic you can use to tap into an awareness that you need in order to deal with certain issues, or to become aware of certain possibilities or people.

But these are my paradigms, and although you will be exploring them in this book, I encourage you to develop your own paradigms of space/time. What matters most is that you create a system of space/time magic that is understandable and workable for you. My work is only meant to inspire and provide guidance. Ideally, the work you do with space/time magic will ultimately culminate like so: "The Great Work of Magic is the collapsing of the future into the immediate present; the magician seizes reality and lives *now*, free from the bonds of his past and knowing that the future is the manifestation of his Will" (Condensed Chaos - 1995, *Phil Hine,* p. 63). The most important thing you can do with space/time magic is to not merely learn how to understand or work with it, but also know when to seize an opportunity, collapse probabilities into concrete reality, and from there manifest your desire, so that you achieve what you need to do in order to advance yourself beyond your current situation. You free yourself from the bondage of space/time by knowing that it is not unchangeable, not set in stone, and can be worked with in a manner that allows you to do more than just bewail the circumstances you are in.

But in order to understand space/time magic, it's a good idea to know the types of magical practices that utilize space/time as part of their medium. Divination is a method of magic that can be very useful for exploring space/time magic and is a good place to start.

Exercises

1. What is your definition of space/time? How much of your life is a linear existence and how much of it is a non-linear existence?
2. I've briefly mentioned my space/time paradigms and Hine's paradigm. Come up with a paradigm of your own that you think would be useable, and compare/contrast it to our paradigms.
3. Think of several situations that occurred in your life around the same time as each other. Were there any synchronicities for you in those events? Did any of your friends experience similar events? Try to explain synchronicity in terms of your space/time paradigm, or use one of my paradigms, or Hine's paradigm.

Chapter Two:
Space/Time Divination

Divination is an art of magic that supposedly tells a person the "future." Many magicians advocate doing a divination before performing a spell in order to determine the outcome of the spell. Others, such as myself, rarely use divination for that purpose. I have my reasons for not doing so, mainly because I feel that divination can obscure probabilities that could otherwise occur, because of a person's willingness to buy into the one, two, or three outcomes that are depicted, and thus lose the various other outcomes that could occur, but are not represented by what is ultimately a limited medium. However, divination, in its various forms, is useful to the creative magician. You just need to take a different approach to how you use divination tools. I only use tarot cards. I know there are other divination systems, but the cards work for me. For those of you who don't use tarot cards, however, it is still possible to take the gist of the ideas I describe and apply them to your divinatory tools.

Perhaps part of the problem with divination is that it might be considered a rather passive form of magic. I put some cards down and suddenly I know my future. However, I have found that divination can be a very active form of magic. You have to do a lot of interpretation, and be open to a lot of possibilities in regards to the interpretation. Divination can be a form of space/time magic. When most people think of divination, they think of tarot cards, or a crystal ball, and a person telling them what will occur in their future. While this stereotype is true of divination, most people don't understand the dynamics involved, i.e. what is actually happening when their "future" is "read."

What actually occurs is not so much a foreseeing of the future, but rather a person choosing to perceive one or two specific probabilities from a field of infinite probabilities. The problem that this can cause mainly comes down to the person choosing to believe in just one probability, as opposed to exploring other probabilities of the future that could be just as useful to them, if they were willing to question what they perceive about their probabilities and the future. Another problem is giving too much authority to the people who tell the "future." By giving those people authority, you give away your responsibility and choices.

In Chaos International # 25, Peter Carroll states that: "With Divination (trying to detect which of the manifold superpositions of the present which actually manifest in the future), things become gruesomely more complicated as the very act of 'looking' seems to act as an enchantment." (Cutting Edge Theory - 2002, *Peter Carroll*, p. 29). Carroll also explains what enchantment is: "Consider first enchantment, increasing the probability of a desired event by will or intent or whatever. The moment of the present consists of a superposition of all possible pasts that could have lead to the present. Some of those superposed states will contribute to the probability of the desired outcome and some will not" (Cutting Edge Theory - 2002, *Peter Carroll*, p. 29). What intrigues me about all of this is Carroll's two positions on divination. First, the stereotypical consideration of divination as an act of looking that is an act of seeing into the future, and second, his acknowledgement that divination seems to act as enchantment. I agree with Carroll that divination seems to be enchantment, and that while many writers and practitioners of magic take the stance of divination being a means of telling the future, others do realize that divination seems to be a powerful, if subtle, form of enchantment. Another take on divination is the following definition:

> Divination is one of the oldest of tools for discovering meaning. To 'divine' means to discover the Will of the Divine (from an ancient root for God/dess, *diew* – shining), and is accomplished by *inspiration* (breathing in), *intuition* (inner teaching), or *reflection* (mirroring). Divination means to

observe signs and see them as symbols, that is, as reflections of higher meaning...Signs become symbols when they point to a realm beyond the objective, tangible world of sensory perceptions...Divination, therefore, involves the apprehension of relationships on many levels. It points to a multidimensional reality [Italics are the author's].

(Tarot Mirrors - 1988, *Mary K Greer*. p. 13-14)

So divination is not just an enchantment, but also a way of working with signs and meaning, of learning to assign arbitrary meanings to events in order to divine what might occur. In order to work with the concepts of space/time magic, most people will start out with a system of divination that on the surface represents a linear model of space and time. Eventually, some people will graduate beyond using the divination systems, while others will continue to use the systems for the rest of their lives. Neither approach is wrong.

First, let's consider the ways you can approach divination as a medium of space/time magic. Gareth Knight's book *The Magical World of the Tarot: Fourfold Mirror of the Universe*, takes a cognitive, semiotic approach to tarot work:

...the intriguing system of interlocking images that can reveal the inner workings of the mind and the world about us. This system requires no special clairvoyant gifts or other rare abilities, simply a knack for using the creative imagination...By these means the Tarot becomes a symbolic language by which we can communicate with a level of consciousness that is different from the everyday mode.

(The Magical World of the Tarot - 1996, *Gareth Knight*, p. 2)

Knight focuses the reader on meeting each of the major arcana in the tarot, thus cognitively working with the level of consciousness the tarot represents. How does this relate to space/time magic? In order to work with space/time magic, you should consider that you are working with layers of consciousness that you don't utilize in your everyday activities. The awareness of space/time must be cultivated by accessing those layers of consciousness through whatever experiences and symbols you can use. Divination is a useful tool for that cultivation, as it gives you a system of symbols, which you can work with and relate to different aspects of your consciousness. For instance, you can meditate on the cards and explore the experiences that the symbols and characters of the cards bring to you through meditation. Knight's book does an excellent job of doing just that, by having a person meditate on a character of the card – The Fool for example – and letting that character give the person experiences that will help him/her understand not merely the symbolism of the card, but also how to work with the influence it depicts.

The practitioner of magic should guard against coming to rely on a system of divination so much that he or she loses perspective. There are several ways to avoid over reliance on such systems. One such way is to be very creative in the various approaches for which you use systems of divination. The other way is to use the system of divination for a period of time and then abandon it in favor of delving deeper into the more conceptual realms of space/time magic (This approach is covered in the other chapters of this book, which present techniques that are not divinatory, and can be used to explore the deeper conceptual realms of space/time, though the magician can continue to use divination along with these other techniques. Ultimately, the choice is yours). You may want to consider abandoning the use of divination because, while it is a potent form of magic, an over reliance on divination will have you have constantly checking the cards before making a decision. Further, by checking the cards all the time you won't be as aware of other factors not necessarily revealed in the cards. Sometimes, you need to experience life without consulting an oracle, if only to fully appreciate the randomness of events and the necessity of being flexible and adaptable to changing circumstances. Either approach is useful, and both approaches will enable you to explore the layers of consciousness that relate to space/time.

More often than not, people will try to memorize the meanings of the tarot cards. This card means this or this card means that. Rarely, however, will people try to define the tarot cards for themselves. But Knight points out that: "…it is not sufficient simply to learn the 'meanings' of the cards from a fortune telling book or instruction booklet that is sold with each pack of cards. We have to meet each face of the Tarot and make it a part of our own experience, just like cultivating a host of friends" (Magical World of Tarot: Fourfold Mirror of the Universe – 1996, *Gareth Knight,* p. 38). In meeting the tarot and the personality that is inherent in the cards, you open yourself to the meanings of the individual cards, meanings that you can understand, based on personal experience. While that personal experience is highly subjective, it can nonetheless be highly useful, not just in discovering the meanings of the tarot, but in delving deeper into the layers of consciousness of which we are comprised. Further, those personal meanings are very useful in terms of working the tarot for probability magic. To illustrate that, Mary K. Greer points out:

> Through a symbol system such as the Tarot, practitioners may discover an inner as well as outer meaning to the words, images and events we experience in our lives. Carl Jung used the term 'synchronicity' to indicate the simultaneous occurrence of meaningfully but not causally connected events. The key…is the word 'meaningfully.' If there is meaning to the seemingly haphazard events of our lives, then this meaning can be discovered by asking what the events symbolize to us. Another way of looking at this is to imagine everything connected with everything else, a living network or giant web, in which the movement of any part is experienced in all parts simultaneously.
>
> (Tarot Mirrors - 1988, *Mary K. Greer*, p. 2)

Meaning is interconnected with events. I would argue, though, that it is your placement of meaning on an event that creates the probabilities that spread from it. This occurs due to the nature of investing meaning into the event. When you do this, you impose your own biases, subjectivities, etc., on that event. These biases shape the event, change it, and bring out certain possibilities that are more likely to occur, while putting other possibilities in the background, making them less likely to occur. The following example illustrates this principle.

If you have a fiery temper, and someone insults you, what is the most likely possibility that will occur? Will you hit that person, or insult the person back? Or will you just walk away? As you think this over, consider that if you have a fiery temper, it will have an effect on which possibilities will more or less likely manifest. Now add in other factors that could affect this situation for you. Is this person a total stranger? Is this person a friend you know, who's not so much insulting you as greeting you? Is this person a hated enemy? All of these factors, these meanings you read into the event, affect it and determine the probabilities that will happen. Of course, the other person also brings his/her own meanings into the events, and this likewise affects the possibilities that manifest into reality. Meaning is also connected to synchronicity. The meaning we place into random coincidences, arguing that these incidents happened for a reason, is called synchronicity. We link these events to ourselves, to other people and events, and use them to justify why such events occur.

Is there really such a thing as synchronicity? Certainly, if it's convenient for the person, if a person decides to manifest the synchronicity by reading into events the meanings that enable him or her to make the most of them: "The tarot reflects our reality back to us! Through it we see what we are creating in our environment consisting not only of the past and present, but the forking probabilities from which we choose our future" (Tarot Mirrors - 1988, *Mary K. Greer*, p. 2-3). The tarot is not only a method for seeing the reality you create. It is a means of creating the possibilities you seek to manifest into reality. By learning to recognize how you use your own biases to read the cards, you can purposely use the tarot to shape events, as opposed to just "reading" them.

A personal example of this comes from a technique I developed for the tarot cards. Once a year on New Year's Eve, I would do a reading that would forecast the major influence for the months ahead. It was a twelve-card spread, each card representing a month. Every year I did this I would note the card and meaning for each month, and then wait and see if the influence manifested for that month. Invariably, the influence for the particular month would manifest, though never the way I expected. Nonetheless, I did recognize the influence for that month once it occurred. But what never occurred to me was that perhaps the only reason the influence suggested for a particular month manifested was because I had been willing to put meaning into that influence, and in doing so set up the probability for it to manifest. Admittedly, the influence of any month never manifested the way I thought it would, but the reading I did was very general, and therefore left room for possibilities in the manifestation of the reality I'd projected for myself through the cards.

In 2002, I decided that I would not do the year reading. I wanted to have more options than that reading would give me, and consequently I had many surprises occur to me. Since then, I've consistently chosen not to do that particular type of year reading, because I don't want to limit myself to a specific influence for a given month. But this year (2005), as a further experiment, I pulled the cards for the year and had someone else turn them up and record the meanings. At the end of the year I'll look at what meanings were written down and see if they applied to this year I experienced. Nonetheless, I feel that sometimes it is better not to know what might occur, in order to increase the probabilities of anything occurring.

Greer uses the mirror as a medium for the tarot: "For me, the meaning lay in the resemblance between the magical mirrors found in many cultures and tarot. Each card represents a mirror of ourselves at the moment we draw it from the deck. The deck itself represents all our probable selves existing simultaneously, but in a sense, not elected in the moment" (Tarot Mirrors - 1988, *Mary K. Greer*, p. 2). Greer's approach to tarot as extensions of ourselves, as opposed to portraying the future, acknowledges that divination is not a linear system that presents one future, but rather a system that has permutations of possibilities. The view that people fall into – the popular view of tarot as a means of reading the future – creates a danger of believing in a specific future that will occur. That future will undoubtedly occur, because the person chose to believe in it, and consequently shuts out all other possible realities that could be. Simply put, you can lose perspective when you are willing to believe that the tarot is telling one specific future, as opposed to representing many possibilities for you to choose from. You need to open yourself to chance, to perspective, to a non-linear consideration of divination and, consequently, space/time. That non-linear understanding of space/time leads you out of the traditional perception of reality as existing only on the level you inhabit. Instead, it opens you up to a multi-dimensional perspective of reality.

In *Tarot Mirrors*, Greer has a number of exercises that I recommend for exploring the tarot as gateways of multi-dimensional realities. One such exercise is the moving meditations, which I did before I read the book. In these exercises you become each aspect of the major arcana via movement. This moving meditation is very enlightening, as you become the tarot card for a time. This in turn opens you up to the probabilities the tarot card represents, because you essentially become the card through the movement.

In another exercise, your emotions and intuition guide the reading of the card. In the summer of 2003, I was feeling a lot of bitter emotions over my financial matters, and this emotional/intuitive exercise not only allowed me to come to grips with the emotions, but also presented opportunities I'd blinded myself to in my bitterness. I picked out cards that represented my situation, how I wanted the situation resolved, what I would do, and factors that could modify how I wanted the situation resolved.

I highly recommend picking up *Tarot Mirrors* as a means of exploring space/time probabilities through tarot.

As I briefly mentioned above, when referring to how people will believe in one possible future, and thus block out other probabilities, belief is the key to the temple of divination. Belief in what you do is integral to making the magic work, but sometimes belief can hinder more than it helps. And in the case of the tarot, where the stereotype of being able to read the future has become so pervasive, belief is much more of a hindrance than a help, unless you are willing to change the belief about the supposed reality of a situation. What you must remember is that beliefs can be changed, and the more malleable you are with your beliefs, the better you are at working magic effectively. Occasionally, it can be useful to believe that the tarot has predicted a specific future, but the reading has to be exceedingly specific to iron out the random factors that can change the probability, so that, while it may occur, the probable future doesn't happen the way you expect. Greer points out that:

> A belief is any idea that you accept as truth, whether it is limiting or spontaneous. Core beliefs are ideas about your own existence that attract supporting beliefs to them. They form the basis of your experience of the world and your way of organizing data. Beliefs function like particles of light in quantum physics: they are true and not true simultaneously. They are true in that you can accept them as truth, and they are not true in that you can change them and their reality. Beliefs are often experienced as fate. By choosing to change those beliefs that limit your experience in undesirable ways, you make your own reality; this is the true secret of creativity and ultimate responsibility of freedom
> (Tarot Mirrors - 1988, *Mary K. Greer*, p. 123)

In other words, we can't cling to beliefs too strongly, or they will dictate our reality. The true power of a magician is in knowing how to change reality to suit his/her needs. Accordingly, we must be wary of any stereotypes that reinforce a belief about a tool of magic. And being willing to change a belief at the drop of a hat certainly doesn't hurt either.

Even with the recognition that the tarot can represent more than one or two futures, you must still be wary of mistaking the tool for the actual practice. Learning to work space/time magic ultimately is done through the magician. The tarot serves as a tool, as an expression of the magician, but precisely because it can limit your scope of possibilities by predicting a limited number of probabilities, you have to be willing to explore alternative avenues of space/time magic. This applies to any tool of divination.

However, before you explore those other avenues, there are some methods you can use with tarot cards or other divinatory tools that can be useful for fleshing out probabilities. These methods are also useful for beginning to explore a non-linear frame of mind.

First, I suggest that the tarot cards you use should have a lot of diverse imagery on them. To give you an example, I use the Voyager tarot deck. The cards of this deck employ a collage technique. You'll see a diverse range of images. For the Emperor card, as an example, there are several human faces, several goats, pyramids and skyscrapers, and a jewel box. All of these images can be connected to each other, but can also represent diverse probabilities. The cards are rich with imagery, and rich with probability. Ideally, the deck you work with will also have rich imagery, and yet be divergent enough in imagery to suggest more than one meaning.

I also suggest not memorizing the meanings of the cards. I've found that the best readings occur through my intuition. You should seek the intuitive impact of the cards, as opposed to a more cerebral understanding of the meanings behind them. In other words, what do the cards tell YOU? When you focus on memorizing the meanings, you're focusing on the words that describe the experiences the cards give you. But can those words alone really tell you the meaning of the cards, or instead can you rely on your intuition of the imagery, choosing to explain the experience through the medium of the words you choose, as opposed to what someone else dictates to you?

You can also use the medium of meditation to explore the cards. Why limit yourself to words, when you can meditate on the images and let those images take you to the field of probabilities concerning the question asked? You can use and manipulate the images of the cards to explore the various probabilities that inform the situation(s) in which you are involved. Ultimately, the most important aspect is to work with a deck that is rich in imagery, with enough variety in that imagery

Taylor Ellwood

to allow for more than one or two possibilities when you read each card. You should also be comfortable with the deck. I have found the Voyager deck to be very useful in the workings I do with it, and I'm very comfortable with it, as opposed to my previous Thoth deck, with which I don't feel as comfortable doing space/time workings. In part, this is because of the imagery, and in part because of the level of comfort. For me, the Voyager deck allows for a wider range of possibilities to be seen in the cards. But for someone else, the Thoth deck might perform that function. It is entirely dependent on you and how well you mesh with the cards you use.

Primarily, you should learn to "listen" to the cards. I always shuffle my cards until I get the message from them (or perhaps from my intuition), to stop shuffling and start dealing out the hand. The second thing to remember, when you see the cards, is that they do not depict the future, past, or present. They can give you suggestions of what *might be*, but nothing is fixed or determined, unless you are willing to invest the energy into what you perceive. I find that by perceiving the cards as giving suggestions, as opposed to dictating a specific future, that I am much more open to alternate probabilities that might not be shown in the cards, but nonetheless can still occur, and thus have an effect on the situation being examined. You may also note that I mentioned past and present. I always find it's best to consider that there are multiple presents and pasts, as opposed to an unchangeable singular past/present. Psychology has shown that many of our memories of the past are "made up" by the brain, which for me suggests some bleed-over of alternate past probabilities. I'll go into this more in the chapter on retroactive magic. Suffice to say that you might wish to consider that there is more than one past and/or present for you, but that you might not be aware of these probabilities, due to the artificial constraints of linear reality. When I use the tarot cards, I consider that each card depicts multiple probabilities and perspectives, and use that to help me gain perspective on how I use them.

The first method I like to use is one in which I draw one card for the past, one for the present, and three for the future. These five cards are merely the start of the reading, however. If you want details or alternate probabilities, simply continue pulling cards intuitively out of the deck. This means that you pull out a card from any part of the deck, as opposed to from the top of the deck. As you look at the cards, write down the impressions you get, focusing on being as specific as possible, but also allowing the raw data to express itself as it will for you. You may find that you don't write anything, but instead draw something. The idea is to follow your intuition, allowing it to tell you what you need to know. Don't try to interpret the cards with the booklet that came with them. Simply experience the cards, and in your own words/imagery translate the probabilities. When you look at the cards, try to consider as well not merely the surface meaning, but any alternate meanings that spring to mind, for either a single card, or for a group of cards. Key yourself into finding more than one probability, considering the cards from more than one perception. Also, ask yourself how well the cards depict the situation. Do you know of any factors that are not presented in the cards? If so, how do those factors affect the probabilities that the cards depict?

Another exercise I like to use with the cards involves pathworking with them. What I mean by this is that you use a card as a doorway, visualizing it in your meditation, and then projecting yourself into it and into the probabilities it depicts. This kind of pathworking is not only useful for getting to know the cards, but also for exploring specific probabilities that you might associate with the individual cards and the position they're in within the overall reading. I usually do this kind of pathworking if I'm unclear about what a card represents. By doing this meditation, traveling into the card, I can experience the message from another perspective, and at the same time explore all the probabilities of the card through the meditation. I also treat the card as a gateway to another realm of existence, and use it to enter that realm (whatever it is) of existence. Here's how I do it.

One spread I use is based on the eight arrows of chaos. One card is in the center, representing the untapped potential of the situation, the impetus to make the situation happen. Eight cards are spread outward representing not eight possibilities, but multiple possibilities, all connected to each other and to the potential impetus. I visualize cords of energy connecting each card to all the other cards in the spread. For the potential impetus, I usually use the Magician card (although you can use any card that best represents the impetus for your working), representing as it does, for me, action or desired action via magic. But that's my preference. On the impetus card I place a piece of paper with my own personal sigil on it, representing my force bonded with that of all the possibilities of the Magician. I usually spend sometime meditating or pathworking with the Magician beforehand, so as to get a feel for how the personality of the Magician card meshes with my own. You can do this with a traditional spread as well. The goal is not just to read the cards, but to interact with them, starting with the card that represents the drive to manifest change, which with my spread is the Magician meshed with myself.

Pathworking is essential with this technique, because it involves using the principle of magical imagination: "The term *magical imagination* refers to the art of changing your consciousness to rebuild aspects of your life and self to bring about a transformation of your environment" [Italics are the author's] (Farrell, 2004, p. 5). You can use the tarot cards as a medium, as doorways to access the possibilities that are around you, ready to be discovered and realized. The Magician is a guide, and each card is a doorway that leads, not to one meaning, but to many. These doorways can lead to each other, because every possibility is related, even if that relationship is one of opposition. You might have realized that eight cards, plus the impetus card, involves a fair amount of pathworking, and you are quite right. It does. This is why my method is different from a standard reading. The process of making the possibility manifest happens through the pathworking done with the cards. You explore as many different avenues of possibility as you feel you need to. Because every card has a multitude of meanings, this can involve some work. It all depends on how thorough you want to be. And, of course, you can always bring more cards to your circle. The real question is how much detail you want to cover. I tend to be fairly detailed, so I'll sometimes include extra cards, or instead focus on soaking in as much detail for the pathworking that I'm doing. I'm also always willing to extend such workings through a period of days. You're not reading a future so much as actualizing a possibility or possibilities. I don't set a specific time period for a ritual such as this, but I will give it as much time as I need to be sure of the details. I know that in the process of the pathworking I'm doing, I refine and shape the probabilities. I explore probabilities I don't want to manifest, and turn them into free energy, which I pour into the other possibilities until I actively arrive at the "future" I want to create, aware, at the same time, of other possibilities that can either help or hinder that "future."

When I'm pathworking, I pay close attention to the card's symbolism. For each card, I take the symbolism I find, and impose a sigil on the doorway of the card. You can physically draw a sigil and place it on the card, or you can mentally visualize it, which is what I usually do. Either method will work. I destroy the sigils that represent the possibilities I don't need, either burning the physical representations or mentally tearing down the door, and then putting the energy toward the probabilities I want to manifest, charging up the sigils that represent the potential realities. You can fire those sigils through sex magic, or whatever other methods you feel are useful in achieving your goal.

As you can see, this technique focuses on working actively with the cards to produce more than one possibility, to achieve perspective, and then push that perspective toward manifestation. Even if you just want to manifest one specific future, it's still important to discover and explore alternate probabilities. By doing so, you achieve a far better understanding of the magic you do than if you just look at one future. Nothing is determined that we cannot ourselves determine, but gathering information helps you decide what possibility is most useful for you. The more aware you are of a variety of possibilities, the less trapped you are in linear time. Through doorways of possibilities, you find the keys to your own empowerment, the achievement of your own realities, the emancipation of your own life from that which seeks to keep you trapped: the dull, boring reality of the mainstream that insists in absolutes to keep you in your "place."

I suggest that you meditate on one card for while, take a break for a few minutes, and then move onto the next card. By taking a break you give yourself a chance to ground. Each time, after you've meditated on each card, write down your experiences in a journal so that you can look at what you've written at a later time. I've always found my writings to be highly useful in making sense of what I've meditated about, and also in understanding situations that later occurred as the cards "predicted." Remember, though, to keep yourself open to other probabilities and perspectives.

The cards are just tools that you can use to access the layers of consciousness in yourself. The cards, and any other tools, are limited by the very medium – symbols – that they are. They can represent something, someone, or an event, but the actual experience and the living through that experience are far more valuable than the tools. By being open to other probabilities, you can change your experience, change the space/time of your reality, because you are open to more than that which is obvious.

There is a final technique I like to use with my tarot cards. Although the cards are symbols, they do embody meaning, essence, and experience in and of themselves. None of us would use the cards or others tools if we didn't assign some meaning to them. The tarot can serve as an evocation tool to pull that meaning out and give it form. I like to think that the meanings of the cards change for each situation that you use them. The meaning and probabilities are malleable, situational, and so when I do the evocation workings with the cards, it's for a specific situation, as opposed to something more permanent and ingrained, such as the words you might find in the little booklets that come with tarot cards.

What I like to do is to call the spirit of the card through the meanings I associate with that card, to address the specific circumstance for which I need that spirit. The card itself is the housing for the spirit. The lifespan of the spirit is the situation and the specific probability I wish to have influenced by the card. Sometimes the card represents the probability, but sometimes the probability that the spirit of the card affects is from another card. The idea is to use the entity you call forth either to push a specific probability into reality, or to alter the most likely probability into one more favorable for you.

For the actual creation of the entity, I usually look at the probabilities I've written down, and then pick the one I want to manifest and make it into a symbol or sigil. I attach the sigil to the card and evoke the entity of the card through the sigil. When the entity has done the work I need it to do, I take the sigil off the card and destroy it, but leave the card for when I next need to do a reading. For more information about entity creation see my co-written book *Creating Magickal Entities*, available from Egregore Publishing.

With evocation, I also focus on directly pulling the concept into reality by visualizing the concept as a possible situation in space/time that manifests through the evocation. I use the evocation to visualize myself living that concept into existence, as opposed to using an entity that represents the concept. A real life example of this practice occurred in January of 2005. There were two conventions, one in January and one in March, at which I wanted to present workshops. I only learned about these conventions in January, and usually booking for presenters occurs half a year in advance. Nonetheless, I was determined to do the festivals. Instead of creating an entity that could evoke the possibility that I would merely be physically present at these festivals, I instead chose to evoke the probability that I would be *presenting* at these festivals. I visualized myself presenting at them, meeting new people, and enjoying myself there. I then projected that evocation into reality, willing the manifestation of this possibility into reality. I used a sigil on The Chariot tarot card as a mechanism to accomplish this evocation. The Chariot represents travel, and the sigil represented the evocation of the possibility that I would be at this festival. I combined the energy of my desire with the symbolism of The Chariot, and pulled the visualization of my travels into manifestation by visualizing the reality I wanted merging into my existing reality, with the sigil and card acting as channeling media. Evocation is a useful tool, and the entities you pull forth are part of that tool. But why work with an entity, or trouble yourself with a bargain, when you can just pull the probability itself into existence? Summoned entities represent the probability you wish to evoke into existence, but if you are very good at visualizing, and you know exactly how you want the probability to manifest into your life, then visualize that instead of the entity, and pull that probability into existence using your sigil on the card as the medium for doing so.

Tarot cards can also be used for very active forms of magic working. A tarot spell, for instance, could involve using several cards in conjunction with each other to manipulate specific probabilities into existence. Each card would obviously interact with the others, so that one probable influence would exert an effect on another influence, and vice versa, but both influences could be used to shape reality into being. And these influences also work with your mind:

> Because there are numerous factors which influence the course of our daily lives, there are multiple probabilities for the directions which our lives, as well as circumstances in general, can take. Among the things which can influence the shaping of events are conscious and unconscious thoughts...The tarot spells provided here will serve as a means for you to focus your will and communicate your desires to your own subconscious, the mind of others, and to the plane of Thought in the language of the unconscious mind – the language of symbolism.
>
> (Tarot Spells – 1990, *Janic Renee*, p. 2)

The language of symbolism, whether through tarot cards or other means of expression, enables you to perceives new possibilities and exploit them. Using a hand of tarot cards can be an active experience, if only because you direct the symbols toward influencing the probabilities you want, and negating the ones you don't want. Simply look at the cards, determine the meanings, and then put the energy of those meanings into your environment.

You can do this by burning candles, coming up with a chant that summarizes the meanings of the cards, or you can do what I do, which is to visualize the spirit of the card and then evoke that spirit into your environment. Give it a specific task and send it on its way to perform that task and create your new reality.

Another technique for space/time divination involves using your television. Ask a specific question about a situation. The TV remote control is your wand. You push the buttons at random to activate the TV and randomly surf from channel to channel. In *The Watchmen,* by Alan Moore, the character Ozymandias has a bunch of television screens set up, so that he can watch all the TV channels at once. He does this to have a sense of the patterns that are occurring in the world and adapt his plans to meet those patterns. Although you might not have multiple TV sets, beyond two or three, you can also do the same thing by channel surfing and being open to the impressions you get. Make sure you keep a pen and paper beside you, and as you channel surf, stop for a few moments and write down what you get, and then move to the next channel. When you are done channel surfing, see what kind of impressions you wrote down and if any of them relate to one another. See if any of the impressions apply to you and your circumstances (they might not). Even if they don't seem to apply, try to see how you could take the probabilities presented in the impressions and use them to your advantage and opportunity in the past, present, or future.

You can also watch a specific program for a few hours. In his book, *City Magick*, Christopher Penczak says: "Not only can we watch images on it [referring to the TV] and feel a connection to them, but, through the VCR and video tape, or even a video camera, we can trap these images in an endless loop for our ritual purposes. The white noise of static can be used to distract our conscious minds during trance work" (City Magick: Urban Rituals Spells and Shamanism - 2001, *Christopher Penczak,* p. 151). You can use DVDs for this kind of work. What I find is that after watching for an hour or so, my attention begins to wander from the show, and at that time I begin to trance out, still watching the show, but not focusing on it too deeply. I also like to fast forward or rewind to random sections, finding this useful as it can "dislocate" me from the linear reality of the show. And that dislocation allows for a deeper trance. Usually this kind of trance wanders from subject to subject. I'm not focused on being specific. I want the randomness, the flashing of moment to moment, as opposed to a definite line of time.

Sometimes, this kind of trance work happens better with a static screen. Chaos magicians, specifically TOPY (The Temple of Psychic Youth), have used the static television as a way of trancing out, or even doing sigil work. You can use a magic marker, draw a sigil on your television screen, and then stare at the static on the screen, using that as a way of charging the sigil. Similarly, you can use the static as a way of doing space/time divination (Penzack, 2001), staring at the screen and trying to find symbols in it, with reference to your questions. However, you should be wary of what you see, as you might project what you want to see, as opposed to what you need to see.

I do want to emphasize two points. First, all of these techniques can easily be used with most other forms of divinatory tools. You might have to modify the techniques, but they are useable. Second, remember when doing any space/time work that you shouldn't focus exclusively on short-term goals. Think ahead to the long term. A situation that might be an advantage in the short term could become a disadvantage in the long term. Learn to think ahead, use strategy, and decide on the probability you wish to manifest, based not merely on short term pleasure, but also long term success.

Exercises

1. Try out the twelve month divination technique. See if your experience is similar to mine, that is, see if the influences the cards depict for each month occur or do not occur. If they do occur, do the influences occur as you expect or not? Why do the influences occur?

2.   Test my hypothesis that belief is what makes a divination reading manifest into reality. Look at past divinations you've done and ask yourself this: if the future that the cards showed did manifest, why did it occur and how? Try some readings now and likewise note the results.

3.   Try to come up with a new divination technique, based on the principles I've discussed above.

4.   Try out one of the space/time techniques. Try to find all the probabilities that the cards suggest are in the situation, in reality, and then try to manifest as many of those probabilities into reality as possible. How does your awareness of the probabilities change them, if they change?

5.   Do some television magic. Use your remote as a wand to open yourself to probabilities that you might not be aware of. Flip through channels randomly, and then write down the images you receive and relate them to an event in your life.

6.   I have my own variation on Greer's moving meditation. I like to assume the pose of the figure in a particular tarot card and use that pose as a way of getting to know the meanings of the card. The Hanged Man, in particular, has provided a very powerful initiatitory experience. Take a card, try out the pose depicted on it, and then duplicate it either standing, sitting, or lying down. Meditate in that pose.

7.   When working with the cards, try looking at them from different angles. Look at the card sideways, or diagonally. Do you find new symbols or does the meaning of the symbols change? Is the position of the card, both in relation to the rest of the cards, and how it is placed, i.e. whether it's upside down, or on its side, important to the context of the actual reading?

Chapter Three:
Retroactive Magic and Perception

Retroactive magic is magic done in the present, but its effects occur in the past, as opposed to the present or future. This kind of magic demonstrates the plasticity of our reality, in that the past is not set in stone or determined, but can be altered with a proper understanding of what is actually being changed.

Reality, as we seem to know it, is not as unchangeable as it appears to be. The reality that we perceive around us is just that: perceived. We have no idea what reality really is. We use our five senses and technology that enhances them to mediate reality. But even if everyone sees the color of grass as green, the shading of the color green might be completely different from person to person. And the act of perception is active: *"Perception does not consist of passive reception of signals, but of an active interpretation of signals"* [Italics are the author's] (Quantum Psychology – 1990, *Robert Anton Wilson*, p. 40). In other words, we actively shape the reality around us with how we choose to perceive it. And how we choose to perceive reality also has to account for how selective we are with the sensations we receive, and how we fit those sensations into the model of reality that is the most convenient (not necessarily the best) for us. Sadly, many people do not realize the responsibility that is involved in actively shaping what they choose to perceive as reality. This is not to say that reality exists only *because* of us. Rather what we *think* of as reality is a perception, but not necessarily what reality might actually be. What we sense is not always what is actually there.

Consider the most recent argument you had with a close friend. What do you think that friend's version of the argument would be? How much would it differ from your version, and which version is "real?" What if both versions are real and equally valid? If you have a witness, what is his/her version of the argument, and how does it differ from your version or your friend's version? What similarities in the version of the witness agree with your version? Likewise, what is similar to your friend's version? Feel free to add more witnesses and find out about their versions. You will likely find that no version is alike, and that each person will swear that his/her version is the reality that occurred. What is reality? Can you really define it? Or at best can you only provide a model of reality, a model that you use to attempt to understand and define what seems to be around you?

> We still assume the 'external universe' from which we started.
> We have merely discovered that we cannot see it or know it.
> We see a model of it inside our heads, and in daily life forget
> this and act as if (1) the model and the universe occupy the
> same area of space (as our map tries to show 'all' about
> Dublin would occupy the same space as Dublin) and (2) that
> this space exists 'outside.'
> (Quantum Psychology – 1990, *Robert Anton Wilson*, p. 54)

If your perception of reality is a model – merely a way of attempting to understand reality, but not necessarily knowing what reality really is – then everything in your model of reality is suspect, due to your reliance on your perception of reality. This includes what you think space/time is. Is space/time really what you say it is, or even how you experience it, or is it more malleable?

Given that you can change your perception, it also seems that you can change your reality. You base reality on your perceptions, so as you change your perceptions, so too does reality, as you know it and experience it, change. Even your memories are changeable:

> Our idea of whom we are is based on memories of our
> experiences, memories that deviate from the actuality of the
> events in question. People who live in the past dwell on
> nostalgic memories, not the minutia of the past...If we can

58

teach ourselves to forge a bond between that feeling of nostalgia and a manufactured memory, we will be able to cause the brain to transcribe the short term experience of a manufactured event into a memory as long-lived, and powerful as the memory of our first love.
(Manufacturing Memories - 2005, *Brian Shaughnessy*, p. 17).

I have often felt that the memories that you or I possess are not just a connection to our past, but also to the multiplicity of the self, i.e. to all the possible versions of ourselves. Through working with your memories you can achieve an effect where you access the memories of other probable versions of yourself and co-opt those memories into the magic you use. This is where retroactive magic comes into the model of space/time magic I'm exploring: "In retroactive enchantment an act of magic alters the probability structure of the ether patterns in the past shadow time of a particular ordinary pseudo time moment. This can result in a subsequent moment of ordinary pseudo time exhibiting a present real state and shadow time future, which may also manifest physically later, which is other than what might have been expected" (Liber Kaos – 1992, *Peter Carroll*, p. 39). In other words, retroactive magic is the shaping of past perception to explore probabilities that can occur in the past. We often think of the past as unchangeable, written in stone, but the past can be changed as much as the future or present can be changed. We simply have to be aware of the probabilities, aware of how to exploit those probabilities. And that requires changing our understanding of the past.

To give a concrete example of retroactive magic, I work with a group of magicians in the United Kingdom, and because I live in the United States, we always have to synchronize our rituals. However, there have been occasions when I haven't been able to do the ritual with my group. On those occasions, though, different members of the group have told me that they could feel my presence. Days later, I would end up doing the ritual and projecting my presence into the past when the ritual had actually occurred for the magical group. That's an example of retroactive magic, where I changed a specific moment in the past by doing something in the present that affected that one moment, creating, in this instance, the probability that the participants would feel my presence while doing magic. Shaughnessy notes a similar effect in his own work: "The memories of the ritual can be placed in the past, effectively causing a retroactive enchantment that produces results in our present. Future memories can also be created for this purpose when we send enchantments of knowledge back through time to our present self" (2005, p. 18). Déjà vu is an example of the future memory principle at work. Each time I've experienced déjà vu, I've noted that the first experience was a daydream in the past, and that the actual experience occurred in my present, but was sent to the past to prepare me for that moment. Usually the déjà vu is an experience of a bad situation, but having retroactively experienced that moment in my past, I am able to handle the present – the actual occurrence – much more easily, because I am prepared for it.

When I work retroactive magic, I focus on a very specific moment in the past that I want to change or work with. I find that the more specific you make the moment, the easier it is to create the specific probability you want to manifest into the past. I do want to offer some caution, though. Doing retroactive magic is not something that should be done lightly. A person I know, who has done retroactive magic, used it to erase a specific occurrence in his life, but found to his horror that in doing this he erased certain aspects of himself. You might think it odd that he'd be aware of this, but an intriguing aspect of working this kind of space/time magic is that you are able to recall what occurred before the change, as well as the difference, or new reality. Carroll points out: "The subtle mental manoeuvres required for retroactive enchantment depend on suspending conscious deliberation and memory, and will fail if you try thinking consciously about your thoughts" (Psyber Magick - 1995, *Peter Carroll*. p. 33). Being conscious of this work can lead to problems you might not be able to resolve easily within your mind. In any case, changing the reality that you were, for a different version, isn't always ideal. The person mentioned above has had to do a lot of work to regain those aspects of himself that he felt were essential to who he is as a person.

With retroactive magic, awareness of all possible outcomes is the key to deciding what you really want to do about a specific moment in your past. How will this moment being changed affect you as you are? Remember that one change can create many more changes as well. The very act of shaping our past, changing what was into something new, also changes everything else we've experienced. My friend certainly found this to be the case, as he realized that so much of who he had been was lost because of the specific moment he'd changed. And though he regained those aspects and experiences that he felt were so essential to him, he nonetheless still does not feel the same, and probably never will. Ironically enough, the one change that did not occur was that concerning the retroactive magic ritual itself. It still existed. If the working *had* ceased to exist, then all of the changes in the past would also have disappeared, as the act of enchantment, of shaping a specific moment, requires that, when the act is done, nothing is changed that would affect the act. That, of course, can create some interesting paradoxes that can screw with your mind and sense of well-being, depending on how reliant you are on being linear.

Despite this need for precaution, retroactive magic is still a very useful tool, and it helps even more when you have the techniques to hone the understanding required to use it. In the example I gave of the ritual I did, all I needed to do was visualize vividly the ritual occurring at a specific time. Then I projected myself into both the visualization and the time. But sometimes a ritual is not what you need or want. Sometimes other avenues are necessary to working and shaping what *was* into what *could have been*.

For instance, divination can serve as a method for "finding" probabilities in the past or future. Remember, though, that the very act of looking seems to shape the probabilities that appear, potentially creating a self-fulfilling prophecy, as opposed to genuine change. As Mr. Carroll aptly notes: "Divinations performed by a magician at (t0) [present(s)] to scry events at [t2] [future(s)] or (t-2) [past(s)] can only succeed if the magician can identify a dominant probability among the plethora of information in either circle. Only divinations that reveal unexpectedly high probabilities tend to count as successes. Note that you can only scry the imaginary past of an event...not the event itself" (Psyber Magick - 1995, *Peter Carroll.* p. 30). In other words, what we divine might just be the probability we *desire* the most, but is it reality or just fantasy, and is the manifestation of the probability fantasy on our parts or a new reality? Does it even matter?

Divination is a convenient tool, and although through "looking" you already shape what you see, if you can manifest the probability into reality – imaginary past or not – the change has the same effect. Perhaps the self-fulfilling prophecy is the means by which reality is changed. Still, the act of looking can change what you perceive you want to manifest, bringing in new variables that you might never have considered. These variables can be useful, but exploring more variables tends to make what you desire less and less probable, as other possibilities spring into chance. Force the hand of chance and make the probability you want into reality. Use divination, if that will help, or other techniques that will bring you awareness of the necessary reality you desire.

Another approach to retroactive workings is to use comics as a tool. I've found ideas that can be adapted and used for space/time magic in a lot of Alan Moore's works, particularly in *Watchmen*. The concept Moore uses does not need to have the format of a comic to be useful, but reading the comic and seeing how the author manipulates space/time via this medium is a very non-linear experience. Part of what creates that experience is the way you physically read comics. Your eyes might range from panel to panel in an orderly left to right manner only some of the time. Some of the comic panels might be arranged for a different kind of reading, in that your gaze has to move around the page in a non-linear way in order to read the story. I find that each comic panel represents a specific moment. You can go back and forth from moment to moment, with each moment coming alive at the time it needs to exist. Because panels are used as the medium for reading, space and time occur together (they do in reality as well, but we separate them by imposing linear reality for ourselves). So the reader experiences nonlinear reality through each panel, which is another reason the technique works so well. Indeed, even how a panel is shaped in comics affects our understanding of how space/time occurs in comics (McCloud, 1993). Most comic book panels are square, but sometimes the shapes are changed to provide a new perspective on a scene. That change in perspective gives a completely different point of view, allowing you literally to think outside the box. And by extension, this can be applied to your understanding of space/time in the sense that your perceptions mold what you consider space/time to be. Reading a comic book is an obvious example of that perception, if you fully pay attention to the dynamics of space/time as it occurs in the comics.

Pick up one issue of a comic and read it. Then consider, as you read it a second time, how the artist and writer experiment with your perceptions of space/time. Do you experience space/time in the way you experience it everyday, or does your perception alter as a result of reading the comic, even if only for a moment?

But let's get back to *Watchmen*. The entire graphic novel is an experiment in space/time magic, with plot twists and seemingly unrelated ideas all converging on a point and referring to other plot points throughout the book. I find this kind of reference to be very powerful, because it shows how magic is connected through the various points of time we live in, how, in fact, *we* are connected through when we live, so that we are living in every moment of time we have ever existed in, or will exist in, even as we live in the present. So how does that relate to magic?

The various connections in the graphic novel occur, not just in the space, but in the *time* of the graphic novel. The reader experiences the past of the characters as the present, and as it relates to the present of those characters. This is significant when the magician realizes that space/time workings delve in all directions of space/time, and will accordingly shape the past, even as the present and future are shaped. The understanding, the perception any of you have about the past, shapes how you view the reality of the present. But the realization that you can shape the past to change the present goes beyond traditional understanding and perception. It goes into your memory. Retroactive magic is worked through the memory of what has happened. Whether the memory or the experience is accurate is a question, but fortunately not a question that affects the magic involved in the retroactive working. If anything, retroactive magic is about changing the accuracy of the moment, changing it in a direction that reshapes reality to your favor.

This kind of retroactive magic is used in issue 9 of *Watchmen*, albeit in a manner that forces the character to face a part of herself she has denied. But again, that's the point of retroactive magic. It reshapes your reality right now. Through the use of comic panels, Moore flits back from present to past to present, getting the character to piece together her memories to the point where she can not only remember the memories, but also change them. Retroactive magic works in a similar fashion. The key is to focus on a specific moment in the past that you want to change.

What I find useful with comics, and specifically with their panels, is how they can be used as gateways. When I think of gateways, I think of portals going somewhere or somewhen else. A magical example of a gateway would be the Tattvas, cards of alternating colors that can be used in trance work to do astral projection or visualization. Likewise, you can use comic book panels, or television screens, or the surface of a mirror as a gateway that can lead you to the specific moments of space/time with which you want to work. Have you ever looked at a television program, or a comic book, or a piece of art, and begun imagining yourself in the world you are looking at? I know I have with *Watchmen*, so much so that I feel like I lose myself in the story, that I become the people I read about and look at. Any time you might have done this, you've visualized yourself into that moment, making the moment part of your reality. And this can be done with past memories as well.

What I like to do is draw comic panels and then put pictures in the panels, looking at the pictures until I feel myself remembering what the picture was about. I allow myself to be drawn into my memory, and begin to experience that memory as my present, living the moment again, and changing that moment if need be. Again, this is possible because any moment we have lived in we actually *still* live in. That moment exists in reality and is accessible. We live at multiple moments of space/time in just one life, and all of those moments are accessible through simply understanding that each moment we've experienced has not *been* lived, but rather *is* being lived by us, even as all the other moments we experience are also being lived. If this boggles the mind a bit, remember that we've imposed a linear structure on our experiences, but that the linear model is not necessarily what we really experience. We use it as a convenient tool to make sense of all the moments in time in which we live.

Another way I use this technique is to watch TV or read a comic and mentally superimpose the memory I want to visit on the medium I'm using to explore my past. This superimposition only requires that you be able to trance, to allow your intuition to flow. I find that space/time workings are very intuitive, very much something that has to be experienced, and not rationalized. Simply change the image and let your mind guide you to the past you wish to go to. You can even use what you do see, i.e. the television show or comic panel, as the kickoff point, trancing into some adventure or news report, and then directing your stream of thought toward the moment of time you wish to experience as the present. In order to activate my intuition, I like to flip pages or channels, and create a sense that reality is not one solid line of time, but many,

> *Everything is recorded.* If it is recorded, then it can be *edited.* If it can be edited then the order, sense, meaning and direction are as arbitrary and personal as the agenda and/or person editing. This is magick. For if we have the ability and/or choice of how things unfold -regardless of the original order

and/or intention over the eventual unfolding. If reality consists of a series of parallel recordings that usually go unchallenged, then reality only remains stable and predictable until it is challenged and/or the recordings are altered, or their orders changed. [Italics are the author's]

(Book of Lies: The Disinformation guide to Magik and the Occult – 2003, *Genesis P-orridge*, p. 106)

Our memories are recorded, but they are more than that. They are when we live. And like P-orridge, I subscribe to parallel realities, to parallel lives. So why not question those lives, find the probabilities, the opportunities we've missed out on, and live them? If we exist in every moment of the life we live, and we have parallel lives, then we exist in those lives as well, and can live them. At that point, changing the reality of the past is much easier than people think. It is the crossing over from one reality to another, or the bringing of probability into this reality. However you choose to perceive it, retroactive magic works so long as you entertain the possibility of it working.

When you close your mind to possibility, possibility stops occurring. How many times have you known someone who had lots of opportunities, but missed out on those opportunities because s/he chose to blind him/herself to them? It happens a lot, because people are so caught up in what they tell themselves about their lives, never pausing to question the validity of what they are saying to themselves. Retroactive magic works for me because I know it's a reality for me, a way of interacting with reality and understanding reality (and myself) better. It's a way to edit reality, to chop it up and come up with something new, or at least to move in a different direction than before.

You never fully realize the extent of the patterns that shape your life, the interactions that affect you and others. I am constantly amazed at the endless amount of bitching and moaning people do about the circumstances in their lives, and their constant complaints that these circumstances repeat. I have to wonder why they can't perceive the patterns that they manifest into reality. They are not victims of the circumstances, because *they* have to do something to bring themselves to those circumstances. But they bitch and blame everyone else, desperately seeking to avoid responsibility. I wonder if their inability to perceive the patterns in their lives is due to the linear reality in which most people delusively believe? I know that if they were to examine their writing or hear themselves speaking, their beliefs about their circumstances would shift, and thus change their reality. All of this reminds me that interaction is an essential part of space/time magic.

For space/time to exist, interaction has to occur, interaction not just with other living beings, but with everything. If you had no interaction, you'd have no perception, no pattern, and no space/time. The interaction you have with a person, situation, or object feeds into your perceptions of ourselves and the situation, person, or object, and consequently forms your beliefs about how you should conduct further interaction. The interactions you have also allow you to shape space/time because the interaction involves intuitive decision-making that affects the interaction's flow:

> The craftsman isn't ever following a single line of instruction. He's making decisions as he goes along. For that reason he'll be absorbed and attentive to what he's doing even though he doesn't deliberately contrive this. His motions and the machine are in a kind of harmony. He isn't following any set of written instructions because the nature of the material at hand determines his thoughts and motions, which simultaneously change the materials at hand. The material and his thoughts are changing together in a progression of changes until his mind's at rest at the same time the material's right.
> (Zen and the Art of Motorcycle Maintenance - 1974, *Robert M Pirsig*, p. 148)

If you realize that no present interaction is absolute as it occurs, but is subject to change as your perception of the interaction changes, then you grasp the basic concept of retroactive magic. And intuition, which does not always require a conscious knowing, is very useful for doing retroactive magic. Your intuition is focused on feeling through the moment, as opposed to rationalizing why the moment is being changed, despite what "laws" of reality say you can or can't do.

Jane Roberts (Seth) points out that the place of power within, time is the present (The Nature of Personal Reality - 1974, *Jane Roberts,* p. 307). The present is your power spot, the moment in which you exist and interact on the linear level. But consider that you exist in all moments and places of space/time in which your essence can exist. This means that the past, present, and future become one, because there is actually no past or future, but rather an unending present, a lateral reality of space/time. And this reality neatly extracts you from the one dimensional perspective you have of time, in the sense that, while you can only experience one "present" moment at a given space, you can move your consciousness through the moments in which you've existed, and make those moments your present.

Retroactive magic is really just placing yourself into a present in which you've existed, changing your perception of that moment, and thus changing the interaction and possibilities that exist through the interaction. You do retroactive magic naturally a lot, whenever you mull over a situation that has occurred before and then change your perception of that occurrence. You change your patterns, and thus your current reality, by reconsidering what you thought of the past situation. You use the present as your point of power, because it is in your present that you change the patterns and probabilities of your past, present, and future, but the present is any moment in which you choose to exist:

> The current beliefs will reprogram and alter past experience. It is not simply that past, forgotten, unconsciously perceived events will be put together in a new way and organized under a new heading but that **in the past** (now not perceivable) the entire bodily response to seemingly past events will change. Your desire or belief will literally be reaching back into time, teaching the nerves new tricks. Definite reorganizations **in that past** will occur in **your present**, allowing you to behave in entirely new fashions [words in bold are the author's emphasis].
>
> (The Nature of Personal Reality – 1974, *Jane Roberts,* p. 293)

From my own workings in retroactive magic, as well as from what other people have said, it seems true that any change in the past will bring about other changes in someone's life, and if they aren't ready for those changes, they could go into shock. Still, within yourself exists the means to manipulate space/time by simply changing your understanding of your interactions, and the patterns those interactions create. The willingness of the individual to change how s/he understands space/time allows retroactive magic to work effectively. You are not stuck in a line that only goes one way. This idea and similar ones will be explored in further detail in later chapters of this work.

Another way you can work retroactive magic is through your dreams. We often dream of events that have happened in the past. This is the brain's way of exploring the past and coping with the stress of everyday life. If you are conscious of your dreams, you can use them to work and shape your pasts. You will need to keep a journal to record your dreams, which will also help you to develop a dream consciousness that allows you to shape the moment being lived again. If you are aware of your dreams, you can change them. People have known this for a long time. Usually this kind of working occurs in lucid dreaming, which is when you are aware that you are dreaming. Your ability to be conscious while dreaming is the key to shaping the moment.

In addition to recording my dreams, I work with an entity of dreams I created called Aloyt. This entity is part of the Dehara magic system that Storm Constantine created around the Wraeththu Mythos. I ask this entity to make me aware that I'm dreaming. Once this awareness occurs, I can change the dream, focusing it on a specific memory that I want to observe or work with. At that point, I reenter the dream, becoming part of that moment and making whatever changes I feel are necessary. Although all of this is occurring in the dream, it still has an effect on the specific moment you chose to work with. Whether you are asleep or awake, you are part of the self that exists in all moments you have lived in and so those moments are yours to remake. As long as you remain conscious of what you are doing, of the moment you are living, that moment becomes the present in which you exist. I find dreaming to be effective for working the changes, because I have deeper access to the storehouse of memory in my brain. I dream the memory and, using my awareness of the opportunities present in that moment, direct the change toward the opportunity that is most favorable. Because I have complete control of the dream, I am able to mold it into whatever I desire. And that dream becomes part of reality, shaping the past into the probability needed, and creating a new present.

When it comes down to it, retroactive magic is about changing your perception. Our understanding of time is limited by our experience of it, but that same limitation can be worked with and shaped, so that it becomes an advantage. Who can really say that retroactive magic can't work? Reality is what you make of it, and that includes not merely being aware of possibilities that exist now, but also those that exist in the past. There is no reason to believe that we cannot shape what has occurred into something else. You simply need to be open to the possibility of doing it.

Exercises

1.   Use the television, comic book panels, mirrors, or tarot cards as gateways to specific memories in your past. Record what happens and how real the experience feels or doesn't feel.

2.   Pick up a copy of *Watchmen* by Alan Moore. Read the graphic novel and try to get a sense of how Moore manipulates space/time.

3.   Record your dreams and try the dream techniques described above.

4.   Come up with your own definition or understanding of retroactive magic, after you've done a few workings. If you're feeling particularly kind, please email me what you've written.

Chapter Four: Sigil Work

One of the best ways to work with space/time magic is through sigils. The contemporary understanding of a sigil derives from the works of Austin Osman Spare: "Spare developed a way of condensing his will so that it was more readily grasped as *a totality*. He did this by writing his 'will' (=desire) in sentence form and by combining the basic letters, without repetition, into a pattern shape, or *sigil*. This could then be simplified and impressed upon the subconscious mind" (The Book of Lies: The Disinformation Guide to Magick and the Occult – 2003, *Neville Drury*, p. 123). When the sigil is a symbol, it is easier to visualize and focus upon. To actually charge and fire a sigil involves projecting the energy of desire into the symbol, then visualizing it in your subconscious, and promptly forgetting about it. Most people burn or destroy the sigils they make. I have a different way of forgetting about what the sigils mean, though I sometimes burn mine as well.

Space/time sigil work involves using sigils for a passive form of magic, or for magic that is time delayed, manifesting at just the right time. As I understand it, most people who do sigil work do it for results, and the sooner the better. I prefer my enchantments to take more time, and accordingly my techniques are based on this principle. There are distinct advantages to my approach. But first I want to discuss the technique of another magician for space/time work.

Phil Hine explains probability scattering in the following passage: "Probability Scattering is a technique which enables the magician to enchant towards low-probability events which lie beyond the possible range of possible options perceived at any one time with reference to particular spheres of operation." (Prime Chaos - 1993, *Phil Hine,* p. 74). Probability scattering is a means of manifesting a probability into reality. The probability needs magic to manifest because it would not occur normally. Hine's technique involves creating a diagram with circles of three different sizes. The idea is to locate the probability in space/time. The circles serve as the scale of high to low probability, and can thus serve as an indicator of how much energy would be needed to manifest the magic. This approach to space/time magic seems linear, in that it charts probability by progression, but it is also accurate in the portrayal of probability, specifically that some probabilities need more energy to manifest than others. The idea, then, is to use the circles as a visual representation of what is needed to manifest the probability, using whatever other tools or techniques are appropriate to it. Sigils are one such tool that can be useful for probability scattering, though again a time delay may occur, depending on how much energy is required to manifest the probability. The Probability Scattering Technique is similar to one of my own techniques, but different enough in overall approach.

My technique utilizes principles of the comic book panels, as well as Imaginary Time. This technique is discussed and illustrated in *Pop Culture Magick,* but it's appropriate to revisit it here.

The essential idea is to use the panels as representations of probabilities you want to imprint on space/time magic. The way panels work in comics is that one panel represents one moment of space/time in the story being told. For action to occur, the reader has to visualize the action occurring as he/she reads the comic. The gap between the panels, which is called the gutter, is where the visualization occurs. Essentially, the gap serves as a link from one panel to another. The gutter, and its role in comics, is best explained as the following: "See that space between the panels? That's what comics aficionados have named 'the gutter'...The gutter plays host to much of the magic and mystery that are at the very heart of comics! Here in the limbo of the gutter, human imagination takes two separate images and transforms them into a single idea" (Understanding Comics – 1993, *Scott McCloud*, p. 66). You visualize the action, the energy, everything that is needed to change one moment into another. With this understanding of how panels work, it's also possible to apply that understanding to the technique of using panels in magical workings. But it should also be understood that:

> These icons we call panels or 'frames' have no fixed or absolute meaning, like the icons of language, science and communication. Nor is their meaning as fluid and malleable as the sorts of icons we call pictures. The panels act as a sort of general indicator that time and space is being divided. The durations of that time and the dimensions of that space are defined more by the contents of the panel than by the panel itself.
>
> (Understanding Comics – 1993, *Scott McCloud*, p. 99)

The panel serves as the medium for imprinting the magician's will on space/time, and worked properly, can bring multiple probabilities into reality at once. You do this by using more than one panel.

Instead of focusing on one probability, you focus on multiple probabilities, no matter how improbable. And instead of exerting a lot of effort to bring that one probability into reality, you use the panels to link each possibility to the other, so that when one possibility becomes reality, the other possibilities are also brought into reality. Think of whatever number of situations you have that need a probability to shape the reality of those various situations. Now draw however many rectangular panels you need to represent all the probabilities you'll be evoking into reality. In each panel draw a sigil that represents the probability you wish to evoke into reality. I like getting colorful with these sigils, and will use crayons and paints as well as a pen. Afterwards, draw lines between the panels, connecting the sigils, with the understanding that when one sigil comes into reality, others will also come into reality. Again, with the lines, be creative with colors. Use colors that create a strong sense of meaning and connection for you. The challenging part comes when you're done with all the artwork. This is when you visualize all of the sigils together, and all of their purposes, as you charge them. Some magicians, after all, will want to charge the sigils all at once. The key, if you choose to do that, is to keep the sigils firmly visualized as you charge them and distribute every bit of energy equally into each. This can be a bit exhausting to do in one sitting. But it can be done, and the lines that you draw between the panels help with that process. Visualize the energy spreading through the lines, into the panels, and onto the sigils.

Another way to charge the sigils is to do one at a time. What I do in this case is focus on the first panel, charging the sigil up and visualizing the energy going into the next panel. The next day I visualize the first sigil again, charging it up, but then visualize the next sigil and charge that up as well, particularly focusing on the energy going from one panel to the next. I do this with subsequent sigils in the series, and when all of them are charged accordingly, I destroy them as I see fit, or keep them, if that suits the nature of the work I wish to do with them, as one can charge sigils again and again, as needed. In any case, charging the sigils doesn't have to be hard.

Nor do the concepts of each sigil have to relate to the other sigils. Each one can deal with completely unrelated situations. The concept of this technique is to free the magician from linear time. The best aspect about it is that when one sigilized probability becomes reality, the other sigils are activated, and those probabilities become reality as well. In this way, you can address multiple situations with one technique. Of course, this technique can easily be modified so that if you want certain sigilized probabilities to occur later than others you can do that, or even perform retroactive magic through this technique, setting it up so that when one sigil is activated for the present, other sigils will affect the past. It all depends on what you decide to build into the working. However, when I charge a lot of sigils, I have found it takes longer for them to manifest into reality. They become time delayed, activating only when the peak of energy is reached, and this can take longer than would occur with a single sigil. But the advantage to this technique is that the overall energy being used to manifest these sigils into reality is much more powerful than that which occurs for a single sigil, and that power is felt in each sigil. Sometimes you sacrifice speed for strength, and with this technique I find that, though the speed of the manifestation is slow, the strength behind the probabilities makes it much easier to manifest probabilities that seem like they will only remotely manifest into reality.

As an example of this principle at work, in September 2003, I did a panel sigil working for a car, as well as the neutralization of a problematic situation with a colleague that had occurred. In April 2004, both situations resolved themselves. It took eight months for the results to manifest, but when they manifested, not only did I get the kind of car I needed – a reliable used car, which needed only minimal repair – but the problematic situation resolved itself in such a way as to ensure that the situation would never happen again. The energy and conditions for favorable materialization of probability had to be built up, but when they were, the probabilities manifested exactly when needed, and not a moment later.

Another approach I take to this kind of sigil working is through paints. I like to paint in the watercolor medium. But instead of creating panels to paint in (though each painting can be a panel in and of itself, so you could do multiple sigil paintings and link them together with pushpins), I like to paint a central sigil that represents the main concept I'm working, and then from there paint other sigils, until the painting becomes a single large sigil containing multiple others within it. I charge both types of sigils by leaving them out where people can look at them. I find that the more attention they get, the more power they receive. The sigils are fired when I forget about what they mean. Instead of burning the sigils, I detach myself from their meaning, leaving the paintings or panels around me, but thinking of them as only scenery, something to occasionally admire. I've found that this method of firing the sigils has worked really well for me.

There are two other approaches to which I've adapted this technique. I also like to use body paints in my workings, and sometimes I'll paint a bunch of sigils on my body and connect them together. In a recent death-rebirth ritual I performed, I painted sigils that connected to each other and represented different situations on which I needed perspective. After the ritual was done, I simply washed the sigils off and let the magic work its course. I found the body paints to be a very intimate way of working this kind of magic, and also felt that the charging occurred not merely through the painting of the sigils on my body, but also through the ritual I did, which involved singing and dancing those sigils into existence, vocalizing the name of each sigil, and then tracing them in the air with my arms and legs.

The final variation on this technique is through collages. I'll cut up magazines, pictures, or any other form of media, and glue the cut-ups onto paper, creating new messages. Each message is its own sigil/symbol, and despite the fact that I use whole words, I've never found this to be a problem for the sigil work I do. The words become part of the sigils, but do not define the sigil beyond any whim I entertain. Multiple messages are connected with lines, firming the intent that reality will manifest more than one probability into reality. I put the collages out where people can see them, and again let their attention charge the intention of the sigils. They are also fired by my forgetting the meaning; they become mere scenery instead of meaningful reality.

Given that these sigils are working on a "timeline," and assuming the probability is manifested into reality, you might wonder if the paintings or panels or collages continue to fire the sigil. I do keep my paintings and some of my similar work, and I've found that even once the probability has been manifested into reality the sigils do continue to collect the energy given to them and then fire that energy retroactively into the manifestation of probability. This retroactive working is extremely effective after the fact, because it does not matter when the energy is collected, so much as how it is used and how well you design the sigils. Simply keep in mind the details when creating the sigil, and if you want it to continue gathering and firing energy into the desired probability, even after it has manifested, then do so.

I mentioned earlier that I do a passive form of sigil work with space/time magic. This is called the sigil web technique. I developed this technique from a pre-writing exercise used to inspire students to write. It is also based on the concept of mind-mapping, which was developed by Lana Israel to help children learn better. Lana Israel is not a mage, but her idea, as well as the pre-writing technique, is well worth using in a magical way.

English teachers will sometimes use pre-writing exercises, and one of these is a web. The web allows a student to brainstorm, but in a way that doesn't require a lot of writing. The web is set up much like a spider web. First you have the central circle. In that circle is the concept you want to write about. On other parts of the paper, you draw lines and circles, and in the circles you write whatever associations come to mind. This helps you organize information. For instance, I could write the word "sigil" in the center and then draw lines to several circles and write "symbol" in one circle and "magic method" in another. Each of those circles would spawn more lines, with more ideas, until eventually you have a page full of lines and circles connected to each other. That's the application for writing.

Mind mapping, on the other hand, recognizes that schools teach children in a linear manner, but that the hardware for the brain is non-linear. The technique of mind-mapping is similar to the web I mentioned above. The difference is that Israel's technique incorporates the use of color as a means of retaining memory of a concept you are working with. It also incorporates the use of symbols that represent a concept for you. The symbols are melded with the colors to create associations within the mind, thus imprinting it with information.

Mind mapping can be very useful for sigilistic work. It works on a similar principle to what I've described earlier, the only difference being that in sigil work the goal is to forget the purpose behind the symbol. My technique for sigil work has melded the two concepts of the web and mind mapping together. As far as I know, my workings with a sigil web of magic are unique. With the web, I do workings that are more concerned with linkage than anything else.

First, I draw on a page a sigil that represents me. This sigil is my essential being. Next, I draw sigils that represent concepts, people, places, objects, and situations within my life. I link these sigils to the primary sigil with lines. I write these sigils down, and draw the lines in one color. I look these sigils over, meditate on them for a bit, think about what they represent within my life, how important they are, etc. Then I decide with which sigils I want to strengthen my connection. I also decide to which sigils I want to cut the connection.

I sometimes end up drawing additional sigils around the sigils I do want to keep. The additional sigils can be used to flesh out the original (and the influence) I'm keeping, as well as modifying the influence. You determine, for instance, if there are aspects of the influence that need to be cut, while retaining the overall influence in your life. For example, you might really like your boy/girlfriend, but feel some of his/her friends are bad influences that affect the relationship. You could draw lines from the sigil that represented your boy/girlfriend to sigils that represented these friends, these bad influences, and then cut them out of your life, while retaining the sigil that represents your significant other. I draw the additional sigils to the primary influence (i.e. sigil) on which they are focused. If you feel you need to strengthen the connection between the tertiary sigils and the primary influence sigil, just do what you feel is appropriate. Some of the tertiary sigils could represent good influences or desired results, such as a raise at your job; you should keep those sigils, so they can modify the primary sigil. The idea is that these tertiary sigils will not merely strengthen the influence in your life, but also strengthen the *manifestation* of that influence, as well as acting as parameters that define the nature of how it manifests.

For the sigils I want to keep I get creative. I might draw other symbols, and/or use colors to represent the nature of the relationship, its importance to me, and in what ways I seek for the connections to be strengthened between my sigil and the other sigils. I put a lot of effort into this work, because I want to represent my needs and desires accurately. Through doing this, I also put energy into the sigils, so in a real sense I'm charging them by doing the labor of love (i.e. art) that I do. After I've cut the sigils out that I don't intend to keep, I either use masturbation or some other way of shedding bodily fluid to fire the sigil. Or I simply tack it on the wall and will the sigils to manifest and then ignore them. Whatever way you fire your sigils should be effective with this technique.

The other thing I do is look at the sigils I don't want in my life. I think about why I don't want them and what they represent. I make sure my reasoning is very clear and to the point. I take out a pair of scissors and cut the sigils. Then I burn them. The act of cutting is the means by which I charge the sigils up with an energy that takes a person or situation out of my life. The act of burning is the firing mechanism for the sigil, the ashes dissipating, and with them the negative influence that affected me.

At this point, I put the web away in a safe place. I will occasionally charge it with energy if I feel I need to. Occasionally, I'll destroy a web and start a new one. Life changes and so my needs change. Using the sigil web is an effective way to work magic. It also requires simple, easily available materials – paper, pen, some crayons, paints, etc, and a pair of scissors – so it's easy on your budget. Also, provided you have the right kind of concentration and ability to focus energy, you should have no problem charging the sigils, or cutting them, for that matter.

This technique can also be used in a group setting. It can be an effective way of developing group communication and resolution of problems, and also just a fun way of bonding with each member of the group. With the group exercise, make sure the magical group is together. I recommend using a large sheet of paper, if possible or, if you prefer, multiple sheets of paper. You can do this technique in two ways with a group. The first way is to have everyone construct their own webs as pertaining to the group, and then have each person explain the various sigils in the web, and how these sigils either help the group or don't help it. Remember, each person will present his/her personal perspective on the group. For this exercise to be effective, you need to be honest with yourself and other members of your magical group. After each person explains his or her personal web, the group as a whole should agree on the sigils to be cut from the various webs and burned. If there is disagreement, this is a good time to work out the situation so that the problem is resolved.

The other way to do this exercise is to have a giant piece of paper. The group as a whole decides what each sigil should be, as well as what it means. Again, honest communication is essential for making the magic work effectively, so the group must unanimously agree on the sigils to be cut or kept. Naturally, the idea of this technique in this case is to sponsor open communication, so that the group dynamics are kept effective and the members stay friendly with each other. Once the group as a whole has decided which sigils to keep and which to get rid of, burn the ones you don't need, and keep the rest in a safe place. Doing this kind of exercise at least once a year will preserve harmony in the dynamics of the magical group. Naturally, however your group decides to utilize this technique, you will also need a group decision on how to fire the sigil web. The charging is done by the communication you put to work in making the group more dynamic than it was.

A few words of warning, though. This form of magic is extremely effective, especially when you use it to cut something or someone out of your life. When you choose to do it, be absolutely certain you want to, because once it's done, it's done. That person, situation, or object never comes back into your life. For instance, I cut a musician friend of mine out of my life. I did this about five years ago, and to this day I have never heard from him and have not heard a word about him from people who know him. And the effect of cutting him out of my life was almost instantaneous. I stopped hearing from him very soon after I did the ritual. Also, if you're cutting a person out of your life, be careful and sure about how you want them removed. If you don't specify this exactly you could end up killing him or her. So be careful and be specific. As you cut the sigil away from the web, you are charging it with your intent.

The other caution is this. It can be hard to cut sigils from the web. A person who experimented with this technique used it to get rid of a bad habit. He told me it was very painful and very hard to cut the sigil away and burn it. He did note that all desire to indulge in the habit stopped soon after the sigil had been burned. Just remember that this can be painful and hard. This is because you are literally and deliberately cutting a connection within your life.

Despite these warnings, try the technique out. It is well worth using, and has been highly effective for me and for those who have experimented with it. It is a useful adaptation of the concepts mentioned above, with my own twist on it. You can use this form of sigil magic to cut away and strengthen connections at the same time. There are other uses for it as well, such as specifying *how* something will be strengthened or cut away from your life. Finally, it's a great exercise in non-linear thinking. You get to perceive how you make connections and interact with people, places, things, and situations all at once, instead of one at a time.

The reason I perceive this technique as being a passive form of magic is that you don't necessarily need to charge or fire the sigils you keep. They represent what you want to keep in your life, but presumably those connections are already in place. However, if you want to activate them, there's certainly no reason why you shouldn't, and occasionally I have done just that. Also, you can modify this technique and include sigils that represent events, influences, etc. that you want to come into your life. Again, that will make this kind of working more active than it might otherwise be. Modify and change as you wish.

As you can see, space/time magic utilizes sigil techniques rather well. The people who have used these techniques have always told me they work exceedingly well, which I think happens largely because of the amount of energy that goes into the sigils. While the sigils require more energy to manifest the probabilities, the results are much stronger, because more than one event is brought into reality. And the best thing about these techniques is that you can set the sigils to manifest at different moments of space/time, but nonetheless they will all manifest as a result of one sigil being activated, thereby pulling the other sigils into reality. The other benefit of this kind of working is that, while results are important, it teaches patience, as well as the realization that everything happens in its own time, as opposed to according to our schedules. In this age of "have everything when you want it," it can be very useful to cultivate patience, when you don't get what you want right away.

Exercises

1. Try out each of the techniques above. Realize that the results might not manifest right away. When the results occur, note down how each of the probabilities manifested, when the probability manifested and if it manifested the way you wanted.

2. Use the web technique to get rid of a bad habit in your life, as well as provide some perspective on the connections you have in life.

3. Try to come up with your own space/time sigil work that is different from my techniques.

4. If you belong to a group, try the group sigil web technique. How honest are all of you with each other? How does each of you react when conflict occurs? How will you use this technique to make your group/community more dynamic?

Chapter Five:
The Magic of Writing

While sigil work has its advantages with space/time magic, there are other ways to approach the system, which also provide some intriguing insights. For instance, writing as a magical art has a lot of benefits for helping you recognize patterns in your life, as well as how to manifest those patterns deliberately.

I've always found the act of writing to be fascinating, and the act of reading equally so. The marking of words can determine reality, simply because people choose to accept the power of the words and what is denoted by them. I've found that writing can be a powerful magical tool for space/time workings.

The word, not god, created the universe, according to the Bible. And for humans, the word is the means of determining the space and time of an event. If I say at two o'clock we'll meet and go for lunch, I'm determining the future, both for myself and for the person to whom I'm speaking, assuming that person wants to meet for lunch at two o'clock. Words define, describe, and explain for us what's happening, who's doing it, etc., but rarely do most people consider how much their choice of words controls their beliefs and the realities with which they interact.

Most people remain unaware of how much power the written word has, and how much power has been invested in it. It has created nations, broken the hold of religion upon people, and otherwise shaped how people interact with each other. Beyond all of that, there are many magicians who use words to work magic. Grant Morrison, for instance, uses writing and images in the hypersigil: "The 'hypersigil' or 'supersigil' develops the sigil concept beyond the static concept and incorporates elements such as characterization, drama, and plot. The hypersigil is a sigil extended through the fourth dimension...The hypersigil is an immensely powerful and sometimes dangerous method for actually altering reality in accordance with intent" (Book of Lies: The Disinformation Guide to Magick and the Occult - 2003, *Grant Morrison,* p. 21). While the term hypersigil might be new, the actual practice is not. William S. Burroughs experimented with how he could use cutup to manifest different events, and also used his other writings as similar experiments or hypersigils to manifest certain probabilities into reality through an extended amount of time.

With writers, I have noticed the phenomenon of the prediction of their own lives in their writing, even though the writing is fictional. And of all the writers caught up in this phenomenon, only William S. Burroughs knowingly controlled the way his writing would manifest his life. Other writers, such as Kafka and Hemingway, seemed to be at the mercy of the words, producing truly great writing, but writing that nonetheless controlled their lives and determined what happened to them. For example, all of Kafka's characters are sickly, working in horrible bureaucratic jobs they hate, or are caught up in a bureaucratic society. *The Trial* and *The Castle* stand out particularly in this regard. Much of Kafka's life was a struggle between writing and working at a job he hated. Yet that is pretty much all Kafka could write about, infusing his writing not only with experience, but also with belief in that experience, and in his inability to escape that particular experience. Not only did his writing predict his own miserable life, but it also predicted the fate of his people. Remember that Kafka died before World War II and the rise of the Nazis, but *The Trial*, particularly its end, accurately reflected what happened to his people. Finally, Kafka predicted his own death in *The Penal Colony.* In that story, people are strapped to a machine that writes them to death. Kafka wrote himself to death, in large part because he was unable to reconcile his desire to write with the job he took and the family he lived with.

Another example is Jane Roberts, the channeler of the Seth Material. Roberts was also an incredibly prolific writer in a number of genres; in fact, she was dedicated to writing to the exclusion of anything else. She developed health problems, and when she worked with an aspect of herself known as the "creator," it became apparent that the creator had inflicted these health problems on her to force her to write. This driving need to be creative, however, resulted in her loss of health, and eventual death. Admittedly, her writing hadn't predicted her health problems, but evidently in some of her short stories she predicted some of the channeling work she did as well as some of her friendships.

Hemingway is also another example. Burroughs points out:

> Nevertheless I think Hemingway came closer to writing himself in present time, closer to writing his life and death, than any other writer...Hemingway wrote himself as a character. He wrote his life and death so closely that he had to be stopped before he found what he was doing and wrote about that...two plane crashes in a row, both near Kilimanjaro. The matador has to smash his head against the window of a burning plane. Otherwise he would have found out why two planes crashed near Kilimanjaro; he wrote it.
>
> (The Adding Machine - 1985, *Willian S. Burroughs*, p 66-67)

Burroughs notes other incidents in Hemingway's life that are eerily similar to what he wrote about. And though Hemingway didn't knowingly practice magic, he nonetheless manifested his own reality through his writing, not merely predicting what would occur to him, but manifesting it through his writing. His writing acted as the medium of reality that would give him so many experiences so similar to his writing. If he had actually known that this was occurring, he could have changed much of the misery that happened in his life.

Science Fiction also provides us examples of where the word brought reality into manifestation. Jules Verne predicted the submarine as we have it now, and the invention of nuclear power and rockets going to moon was predicted in various pulp magazines decades before the actual manifestation of those inventions. It could be said that those events occurred because people read the stories and were inspired by them, enough to go out of their way to bring those realities into existence. The word shaped their minds toward what was, and even now is, invented.

We have only to look at other books, such as *1984*, by George Orwell, which predicted the totalitarianism we see in the United States with the Patriot Act and the suspicion of terrorism at every bend. And for that matter, *The Handmaiden's Tale*, by Margaret Atwood, is a precautionary story. You have only to read it to see that the circumstances that could create that particular future are already in place within the United States. We can, of course, change the circumstances of any of these probabilities, but we have to understand how the word works and the power it can have, through the power people give words.

Still, for the writers who do write and know the power of the word, there are ways of knowingly shaping the writing you do, and thus the reality you create for yourself. Morrison, with his hypersigil, has done this in his writing and work: "My own comic book series *The Invisibles* was a six-year long sigil in the form of an occult adventure story which consumed and recreated my life during the period of it's composition and execution" (Book of Lies: The Disinformation Guide to Magick and the Occult - 2003, *Grant Morrison,* p. 21). But the writing with which you shape reality shapes you as well. By knowing how the writing affects you, you can direct those shapings toward ends that are more useful for you, as opposed to living a Kafkaesque or Hemingway style of life, at the mercy of the writing you do.

Burroughs is another author who used writing to shape his life in directions that he wanted it to go, through the experiments he and Brion Gysin performed with words, using endless collages, and exploring the effects words had on people. Once you realize words can shape a person's reality, you also realize just how much they've shaped your own reality. Burroughs, accordingly, was very well aware of words, and of how he used them to represent his own reality. All of his writing reflects not merely the adventures that his characters had, but the real life experiences that he had. He was very aware of the patterns that his writing presented to him, the patterns of the life he was living, and accordingly he was able to shape those patterns to some degree. None of us as writers ever completely shapes our writing. We shape and are shaped by it. Burroughs knew this, recognizing how viral the word can be.

And how is the word viral? I'm in an academic program that emphasizes the need for definition. Consider that defining something – anything – is a way of controlling what something appears to be. If you can say that something is "this" and get other people to agree with you, you are spreading a virus, albeit one of definition. The definition is just a model of reality, but this is why so many academic articles are written with lots of hedging and defense. To appear certain is a crime, unless you buttress your certainty with a fortress of words and citations, the majority of which most readers won't understand (a specialty of academic writing, and a way of controlling who has access to information). Of course, such practices aren't limited to academics. Within any organization, there will be sub-organizations and subcultures. In these subcultures, the way words are used will only be understood by the insiders to that subculture. For instance, I haven't a clue what most Thelemites are talking about with their numerical references such as 93, 696, and various other buzz words that are part and parcel of their subculture. Were I to join the OTO, I might eventually come to understand the entirety of the meaning behind such words, but as I don't engage in their practice, for all intents and purposes I'm not part of their subculture (Wenger, 1998, Hebdige, 1971). What academics and most writers forget is the following:

> Whatever we look at, we must see, first and foremost, our own 'mental filing cabinet' – the structure of the software which our brain uses to process and classify impressions. *By 'software' I mean to include our language, our linguistic habits, and our over-all tribal or cultural world-view*-our game-rules or *unconscious* prejudices-the tacit reality-tunnel which itself consists of linguistic constructs and other symbols. [Italics are the author's]
> (Quantum Psychology – 1990, *Robert Anton Wilson,* p. 48)

In other words, the language we use, the way it is constructed verbally and through writing, shapes our understanding of the world around us, shapes our reality. The definition can be a virus, because so many people buy into the defining without questioning the reasons behind the act. We control you, who allow us to tell you how reality is. And don't you forget it. (On a humorous aside, you might notice I'm using citations, and that my writing is at least partially academic. I'm happy to use the techniques of others if it proves useful in making a point).

Some of this control is a result of memes, the replication of concepts through language. Commercials are a good example of memes. Everyday, most people watch and listen to them and are shaped by the commercials, suddenly feeling an urge to go out and eat, or go and buy a new music CD by a particular artist. And yet memes are not the only reason that people buy into the definition of words, and themselves through words. The interaction that people have with each other through words also plays a role, in that people use words to get what they want, to reinforce social boundaries, and define the reality of other people around them.

However, although words can shape reality, and can manifest particular probabilities into reality, it's important to know that it is not the words in and of themselves that cause the probability to occur. It is our choice to believe in those words, to give them power, which creates the realities we manifest in our writing. Recognizing this point is very important if you want to use writing as a way of shaping space/time for yourself. Wilson argues: "Words *do not equal in space-time* the things or events they denote, yet people react to a choice between words as if making a choice between 'real' things or events in the existential world [Italics are the author's]" (Quantum Psychology - 1990, *Robert Anton Wilson,* p. 85). While Wilson is quite correct that words, in and of themselves, do not denote the actual events they describe, he does not recognize that words can shape reality – shape space/time – through people's acceptance of the meanings of the words, as well as the interactions that are created through words, between people and people, places, and events. And because the usage of words in spoken and written language seems to be an intrinsic part of human existence, most people do not necessarily realize the power they give words, particularly the written word. What people need to realize is that, while the word does not describe the experience, it can be used to shape the experience and manifest a particular probability into reality.

To that effect, let's consider that writing can produce patterns of probabilities that we can observe over time. These patterns are subjective. When we find them, we create synchronicity in the events we read/write, and yet these patterns can deliberately be created to lead people toward certain conclusions or probabilities, while leading them away from other probabilities. For instance, consider the problem-solution pattern: "The chapter attempts to examine the way in which monologue structures are efficiently signaled to listeners or readers. It concentrates specifically on the way in which a particular English discourse structure – the problem-solution structure – is signaled by *means of questions and items of a particular type* [Italics are mine]" (Advances in Written Text Analysis – 1994, *Michael Hoey,* p. 26). Now, if such structures are used in writing (and they seem to be), consider how this affects both writer and reader, especially if the writer isn't knowingly aware that s/he is utilizing this kind of pattern in writing. A project I completed for a linguistics course involved trying to find this problem-solution structure in short newspaper articles. I ended up finding variations of the writing pattern in the short articles I examined. The pattern of writing, incidentally, is where a problem is stated and then a solution is found. Given that various writers wrote these articles, what stands out to me is that the writers and readers seem to be shaped by what is written, and specifically by the pattern of the problem being stated and the solution being the one that was utilized by the writer! Although the words might not accurately represent the experience that occurred, they do shape people's understanding of the experience, with a specific reality in mind. In other words, because readers and writers are conditioned to specific patterns found in writing, the way they perceive reality and the possibilities inherent in reality is limited by those very patterns, which consequently limits what the reader and writer can do. If you are caught in a pattern and you aren't aware of it, it's hard to know of possibilities outside it, but which are nonetheless just as viable as the ones presented and contained within the pattern of writing being written or read.

This is just one pattern that is used in writing. There are, most likely, more patterns of writing out there that people use each day. Think, for instance, of a cover letter to a company. How is it arranged? What should it say? Usually, there's a formula to different kinds of writing and that formula, to some degree, dictates the thinking processes that shape the writing. In turn, the writing refines the thinking. Is it any wonder, then, that writing has such an effect on people? It might not adequately represent experience, but writing does shape how we understand experience, and can shape the experiences of our lives: "Rather we actively *create* our impressions: out of an ocean of possible signals, our brains notice the signals that fit what we expect to see, and we organize these signals into a model, or reality-tunnel, that marvelously matches *our ideas about what 'is really' out there* [Italics are the author's]" (Quantum Psychology - 1990, *Robert Anton Wilson,* p. 114).Writing is part of how we actively create our impressions, transforming the signals we receive into words, not just physically, but also mentally. Take a look around you at whatever you see, and then describe how you thought about what you saw. Chances are that at least part of your thinking was in words. And there's nothing wrong with this, so long as you are aware of the power of words in your life, of how they can be used to shape and condition your perceptions of reality. If you know the power of words, you can begin to use them knowingly, in a manner that allows you more control over how the reality you perceive is shaped by you.

You can gain more control through manipulation of the word and/or image. Burroughs knew this: "The word, of course, is one of the most powerful instruments of control as exercised by the newspaper and images as well, there are both words and images in newspapers…now if you start cutting these up and rearranging them you are breaking down the control system" (The Job – 1969, *Daniel Odier,* p. 33). The system of control within words, the definition virus, the need for certainty, can all be broken through cut-ups, through collages, even through writing that has no specific goal, but is tangential, intuitive, going where the mind wills. The goal is not to be controlled, or even to control, though certainly as I've said above, awareness of patterns can lead to more control. But the goal ultimately is to break the control of words upon us, to break the definition virus and create uncertainty. And through uncertainty, you can find glimpses of the future. Though again, the same can be said for awareness of patterns in writing. BUT, the difference is that, with specific patterns of writing, you are still operating in the control system devised by other people or institutions. Uncertainty is preferable for written space/time magic.

The reason Burroughs was able to pick out Hemingway as a writer who wrote his own reality was because he had a keen understanding how even the rearrangement of words could lead to a shaping of reality:

> I would say that my most interesting experience with the earlier techniques was the realization that when you make cut-ups you do not get simple random juxtapositions of words, that they do mean something, and often that these meanings refer to some future event. I've made many cut-ups and then later recognized that the cut-up referred to something that I read later in a newspaper or in a book or something that happened...Perhaps events are pre-written and pre-recorded and when you cut word lines, the future leaks out. I have seen enough examples to convince me that the cut-ups are a basic key to the nature and function of words.
> (The Job – 1969, *Daniel Odier*, p. 28)

Like Burroughs, my own experiments with cut-ups have yielded glimpses of future events and have even acted as retroactive forms of magic, rewriting past events within my own life. If cut-ups can offer glimpses, they can be used to do more than that, thus my work with collage sigils, focusing the collages on specific occurrences I want to shape in space/time, and using the words and images to help in that shaping. You can break the definition virus, and capitalize on the probabilities that word and

91

image provide to describe specific probabilities you want to manifest in your life.

The key to writing as a form of magic is this: writing operates as a recording, albeit a biased recording. Objectivity is lost, no matter much you might try to make the wording you use "scientific" or empirical. After all, you're trying to prove something, and when you give meaning to word and number, image and concept, those meanings are biased in your favor. As an example, in academia one of the practices in reading an article is finding the "gap." This involves finding error, finding some hole in the ship that hasn't been patched. This gap leads to further writing opportunities, further research, which is the lifeblood of academia. And for that lifeblood to be sustained, no matter how obfuscating or scientific the writing is, someone will find a gap. That's magic in and of itself.

But going back to the recording, the fascinating thing about it is that it can be changed. Burroughs did a lot of experiments with tapes, cutting up sound, and a lot of musicians carry on that tradition. For Burroughs, it was a magical operation. Perhaps for some of the musicians this is also the case: "Further if all we imagine to be reality is equivalent to a recording, then we become empowered to edit, re-arrange, re-contextualize and re-project by cutting-up and re-assembling our own reality and potentially, the reality of others. If this is true and effective, then a magical act is taking place" (Book of Lies: The Disinformation guide to magick and the Occult, - 2003, *Genesis P-orridge,* pp 110-111). Granted, this is just a paradigm, and yet it does imply how much of an effect that writing can have on people. The amount of information spread by writing, and how that information shapes the reality of people, is not something to be ignored. And whether you call what occurs magic, or something else, you do need to acknowledge that the medium of words can be used as an effective way of working magic.

Let's consider how words are used to work magic. A sigil, after all, is a compressed word or sentence that represents a desire that is being imposed on reality. Words are double-edged, however. While they certainly can represent our desires and needs, they also work against us sometimes, limiting and defining what we wish to represent in ways we don't expect. Let me give you an example.

I have written *The Cut-up Commodity* and am at work on *The Cosmic Collage*. These two books are personal journals, mixed in with observations of society and magical experiments. I hope one day to have them published. In writing the chapters, I have noticed some intriguing phenomena that have involved writing and space/time. When I start writing a new chapter, I pick a title for it. Throughout the chapter, the contents based on what is currently happening in my life resonate with the title. In fact, the events in my life line up with the title, and so I am influenced by the meaning of those words. Certainly, however, I also influence those same meanings, so that in effect what is occurring is a localization of particular influences brought about by the meaning of the words in the space/time in which I am involved while writing that chapter. I am influenced by and influence those meanings. But here come several quandaries. Does this happen because I believe it will happen, based on prior experience with the power of words? Does this happen because the choice of words, whether for title or material in the chapter, defines me for that particular space/time, even as I in turn define those words? I'm honestly not sure, but having noted this phenomenon in other writers, I suspect it is the latter, as opposed to the former. All of us work with words every day, defining and being defined by them. We are essentially textualized by how we choose to use words to convey our experiences.

As an experiment, try these two exercises and note the effects. You will need to start a personal journal, if you have not already. For the first exercise, write a chapter, but before writing the chapter, make up a title for it. When writing the chapter, don't focus on every detail. Write what is notable or intriguing to you, and write this chapter for however long you need to. I can spend up to three months (if not longer) on a particular chapter. When you have finished writing the chapter, read through it and note whether the title has influenced the writing and/or your overall experiences while you were writing the chapter.

For the second exercise, write another chapter, but this time don't pick a title for it. Write the chapter, and after you've finished, wait for a few days, and then give the chapter a title. Now see if the title, writing, and experiences are similar to or different from each other. The purpose of these exercises is to explore the influence of writing in your life, magical or otherwise, and how that writing does or doesn't manifest realities. I have purposely written commentaries directed toward specific needs in my writing, and have found that the desired result is manifested; the writing conveys the necessary force to manifest desire into reality. Even when I have not included a title, I've still nonetheless found a specific recurrent theme in my writing. Sometimes I shape that theme, but sometimes the manifestations occur in ways I don't expect. This shows me that, even as I shape the writing, it shapes me. But don't take my word for it. Try it yourself.

Another fascinating aspect of writing as a form of magic is how it can be used to cut someone out of your life. You can use cut-ups or your personal journal. Look in your journals and see if there is a name of a person you want out of your life. Stop writing about that person. Get rid of the name and visualize as you do so that the person no longer exists, no longer has reality. For you, that person likely will cease to exist. I find that only the really meaningful people in my life show up in my writing again and again. The rest fade into the background and eventually disappear. A person or two may cause a stink for a time, but they only have power so long as I give them power, and I find that removing that person from my writing allows me to take that power from them. Writing is about meaning, so take away the meaning. And remember as well that you can do the same with probabilities. Even as you write some into existence, you can write other possibilities out.

One intriguing aspect about writing and magic is that with writing you can write other realities into existence, or become aware of them, depending on how you perceive the matter. What I mean by that is that I think when a writer writes about a fantasy world, s/he is either creating that world in alternate reality, or, more likely, tapping into that alternate reality. As a good example of that, Storm Constantine's work with Wraeththu has certainly allowed her to tap into another reality. What's intriguing is that people who haven't read her books, but who have worked with the Deharan (Wraeththu) magic, have mentioned that they've worked with this energy before, that it feels familiar to them. It's my thought that writing, being a very intuitive practice (when done creatively), leads people to tap into other realities, other versions of the self. Writers often say that the characters they write about sometimes represent different people in their lives, as well as themselves. Some writers also note that characters seem to be alive and have their own personalities, which consequently affect their writing. Perhaps this is because they have actually connected with an alternative self, and are transcribing that self's experiences into writing that we consider fantasy or SF. In contacting this self, the author becomes a medium for a polyphony of other characters, transcribing the voices of many into the reality of the word. If we bear in mind that writing does shape the realities we manifest, then we can also consider that sometimes the writing is purposely directed toward a specific probability that needs to be manifested in reality. The writer must be aware of how his/her consciousness develops the writing, so that s/he can shape the writing, and the probabilities it creates, toward specific goals that are concurrent to what s/he needs to manifest into reality. In this way, the probabilities we manifest will accurately reflect our needs, as opposed to what any alternate version of our self might wish for.

Writing, and some of the other activities mentioned in prior chapters, can get you in touch with what I call intuitive consciousness, the consciousness that relies on intuition and uses it to surf the probability waves of reality. Your consciousness is a tool. In Western societies, we often value the rational/logical/so-called scientific mindset, but this mindset is outmoded even in science, where contemporary physics show that what we perceive is what we make into reality, despite what logic might tell us. The intuitive consciousness is the consciousness that is in touch with our environment. It helps us navigate through life and the probabilities that we are aware of, and even some we're not aware of. Logic has its place too, as a tool that helps us hone our intuitive consciousness, with which we can connect with other people in ways that logic doesn't allow. Your intuitive consciousness is your gateway to the universal consciousness you share with everyone else; writing and other tools you use are ways of accessing that gateway.

There is one other magical technique that applies to writing, and that is creating your own alphabet of desire. Stephen Mace explains what this alphabet is:

> The 'alphabet of desire' is Spare's name for the collection of symbols or 'sacred letters' that every sorcerer who persists in the method [he's referring to automatic drawing] must eventually design. Each 'letter' represents a power or, as Spare called it, a 'sex principle,' an unconscious structure or a variety of energy that the sorcerer recognizes or wishes to recognize within his deep psyche. The letter acts as a way of designating the nature of this force even while one's rational mind is left in the dark.
>
> (Stealing the Fire from Heaven - 1984, *Stephen Mace*, p. 34)

This alphabet is highly personalized, allowing you to have your own system of words or symbols. The benefit of this is that these symbols have been created by you, and are infused with personal meanings. This means that they will resonate strongly for you, more so than more traditional symbols. The downside, however, is that it's likely no one else will know what the alphabet means. Your alphabet of desire is not meant for communication with other people, but rather communication with the desires within yourself. The difference between such an alphabet and sigils is that the symbols created for the alphabet are used again and again, whereas sigils are usually only used once. Also, the creation of the alphabet is achieved through drawing, as opposed to compressing a sentence into a symbol. Nonetheless, the relationship between your alphabet and your writing means that you can explore some of the ideas I mentioned above, by creating your own language and experimenting with how these concepts manifest through that language.

96

To create your alphabet, focus on one subject, for instance, the emotion of happiness. Think about how you feel when you're happy. Think about the word happy. Then start drawing, and don't try to control the drawing. Just draw until you're done, and then look at the symbol. If you're not quite satisfied with the symbol, start over and see if you draw the symbol for happiness in a similar manner to the first symbol or in a different manner. When you've completed the symbol, you may wish to use some other system of symbols to confirm that the symbol you've created represents your desire for happiness. I'd use my tarot cards, in this case. But you can also base your understanding of the symbol on your intuition of it. Use the symbol to represent happiness for you, and determine from the usage of it if happiness is produced. If it is, then the symbol works. You use the symbol by making it part of your writing, or putting it in a place where you will see it and draw from the desire it represents.

Ultimately, I think that writing can be used to work with space/time because it allows us to organize space/time, not so much in linear terms, but rather in situational/probability terms. I need such-and-such to happen, so I'll write about it, and in doing so, fully express my need. Admittedly, a sigil might be an easy way to compress that writing, but the sheer act of writing is expressive and powerful in and of itself, and sometimes more beneficial for manifesting particular needed results.

Exercises

1. Do all the exercises I've written about in this chapter.
2. Read *The Job: Interviews with William S Burroughs* by Daniel Odier, and *The Adding Machine* by William S. Burroughs, to get some insights into Burroughs's writing and the magic involved in it.
3. Read any books by Ernest Hemingway, Franz Kafka and an SF author of your choice. What do you think about my claims about how these writers shaped reality with their words? Do you agree or disagree?

4.   Create your own alphabet of desire, and superimpose some of these exercises and concepts into it. Record your results.

Chapter Six:
Space/Time Magic and Art

When I was eighteen, I went to an auction house in Pennsylvania. A lot of different items and articles were being sold. It was a fascinating place, but there was one item that particularly struck me: a painting hung on the wall. It had a purple background, the sun sinking into the sea, and an island with a palm tree on it. As I watched the painting, the palm tree and the sky within the painting appeared to move. I felt that I could have walked right through the frame into the painting and find myself in another space and time.

I have since then come across other paintings that evoke similar responses, and no doubt some of you have as well. Perhaps you have been at a museum, or over at a friend's house, and you've felt a piece of art reach out to you and draw you into its world. Genesis P-orridge, who owned a number of Austin Spare's paintings, noted:

> In the same mysterious way that, if you will, a mirror can contain all that it faces in what seems an equally 'real' world, so Spare's pictures can hold the entirety of the images and entities that he represents in them. They are there. The frame is exactly intended to be experienced as, and function as, the edges of a mirror, although, because it is a plastic, more fixed medium, we often cannot see around the inside edges by moving, as we can with a mirror. Do not be fooled by mundane physics. There are specific periods, when, remarkably, the opposite is true, and these images do indeed become exactly the same as mirrors, representing an entire portal into a parallel omniverse...They become living portals

that animate, through which entities can travel, accessing our
'world' and bidding us into theirs.
(The Book of Lies: The Disinformation Guide to Magick and
the Occult -2003, *Genesis P-orridge*, p. 129)

And if these entities can come out into our world, it also stands to
reason that we can do the same, traveling into their world, using
the artwork as a portal to access the energy of the world being
depicted. I have found this to be true with many of the paintings
created by other magicians. For instance, Todd Heilmann, who
did the cover art for Pop Culture Magic, has created paintings
that have always evoked a specific energy for me. They put me in
touch with both the scene and the entities depicted within it.

I also paint, using water color as a medium, and I have found
that while painting, the energy of the act has been charged
through the paint, so that the paintings become alive, charging the
room with their energy and drawing people into the reality they
depict. Sometimes, the paintings also act as a means of
invocation, where the entity is invoked into the person by the act
of attention being given to it.

Similarly, when I've used body paint, I've always felt that the
paint is a medium for the energy to express itself, and that the
painting is a ritual. The painting draws the energy to it, and the
symbols on the flesh are created as a way of channeling that
energy into specific intentions. My body as a canvas, nonetheless,
also becomes a portal for the energy to flow through. And with
the creation of a gateway, art becomes more than just an aesthetic
pleasure, or even a message. It functions as a pathway to access
space/time, to explore probabilities, and to manifest these
probabilities into our "reality."

I always find the act of painting to be one of intuition. I've
never purposely picked out colors, so much as let the colors
speak to me. The painting itself becomes an active participant in
its manifestation of reality. The painting and I act interact in the
realm of abstraction, and together make the concept into reality. I
am the medium, the guide by which the portal, the entity, the
magic is manifested. Accordingly, my paintings have ranged
from being very abstract (similar to the kind of paintings done by

schizophrenics, or so I've been told!), to being more concrete and realized, and yet nonetheless not set in this reality. What I seek to depict is not here; it's elsewhere, in my consciousness, perhaps where my consciousness interacts with other forms of consciousness. The painting is part of me, but it goes beyond that, acting as a way of drawing forth what I have contacted or interacted with. My paintings act like a lens:

> Time is, you see, a solid through which all passes, all is seen from a vantage point. As we learn to move our point of perception, so we act like a lens, or a mirror's surface viewed from above. Light, thought, life, passes through us, expanding outwards. We can place our mirrors anywhere, perceive them from any direction, thus we are potentially everywhere, in every possible time and every possible dimension. All travel is possible. We are an amorphous infinite density of matter. The matter is time. It is all a matter of time. Time is malleable and thus both the portal and means of travel. We can leave, we can return, we can cease to exist.
> (The Book of Lies: The Disinformation Guide to Magick and the Occult -2003, *Genesis P-orridge*, p. 130)

The painting becomes the mirror and the pathway to space/time, to other realities. Consider, for instance, when you buy a book. What draws you to buy a book? It's not usually just the content in and of itself. You might flip through the pages and read what's inside, but the portal to the book is its cover, and the art on the cover acts as a medium to draw you into the reality of the book. And in the case of fiction books, the characters of the story are often visualized through the medium of the cover art.

This medium doesn't occur just in cover art or paintings. Comic books, as I've noted in previous chapters, also do a lot of experimentation with space/time magic, and this experimentation has a similar effect on the reader. Consider the layout of a comic: panels or squares of reality separated by thin white gaps. Each panel acts as a doorway into another reality, and successful entrance into the reality is fully achieved by linking panels to each other, so that the action is read into existence. This reading occurs not merely through the words, but also the art, which in and of itself is a symbol. Indeed, the act of mediating an artwork involves recognition of symbols, which represent abstract concepts into concrete reality: "The panel acts as a sort of general indicator that time or space is being divided. The durations of that time and the dimensions of that space are defined more by the contents of the panel, than by the panel itself" (Understanding Comics – 1993, *Scott McCloud*, p. 99). As with paintings, the frame and the canvas of the comic book is where the content is placed. The frame acts as a medium of time, providing a static moment for you. But you bring that static moment alive in the mind's eye, and it is also brought to life through the intent of the medium expressing itself to the reader. The reader and the comic book interact with each other. The comic is not a passive collection of pages, but an active participant of reality manifesting. And this is also true of other artwork. The ideal artwork is not merely something your eyes experience, but rather produces such an evocative experience that you can experience it with all of your senses, become part of the art, part of the space/time you witness. And at the same time, you move beyond space/time.

Art and writing create timeless space for you. They are, in fact, the most concrete forms of timeless space. Your conception of space/time is limited, based on your perceptions and ultimately suspect. But art has a way of taking you into another realm, providing you with a still moment that can only be brought to life by your perception and your ability to mediate that perception, shaping it into new experiences. Art and words suggest that time is more than just linear, more than just event following event. And the artist who can grasp this understanding can bring that back to the reader/viewer: "Time is not however linear, all time exists simultaneously and points in every direction simultaneously" (Book of Lies: The Disinformation Guide to Magick and the Occult – 2003, *Genesis P-orridge*, p. 136). The painting, the comic, the word, gives you a gateway to access all those points of time. The painting, like a mirror, slips you past the border, past the edge of what most people consider time, and takes you to a new world, a new reality. You just have to open yourself up to the possibilities, as well as move beyond what is often dictated to you, as to how you should react to art, word, or other forms of creative expression.

Creative expression connects you with other layers of consciousness. And it is through that connection that you access space/time probabilities and manifest them into reality. I paint intuitively, flowing with the moment, not consciously trying to control the painting. I think what I find most intriguing about my own artwork is how readily it forms into symbols, becoming sigils within sigils, focusing intent, and yet that intent is being transmitted through an altered state of consciousness. You don't need psychotropics to reach that state of consciousness. You just need to let go of control. I often think that the reason so many magicians use psychotropics is because the ability to lose control, to not be a control freak, has been taken out of us by an increasingly stressful society.

Let go of control. Pick up a brush and some paints and don't think. Just do. There's no definite image you need, no specific masterpiece. Just paint. Let your mind become intuitive, and you will find as you paint that your mind opens you up to a variety of probabilities. Random situations, to which you might not have put much thought, will come forth. Don't focus overly much on them, but keep painting, and let your intuition take you through the probabilities. You will find that those probabilities are expressed and manifested into the painting itself. As you get used to the intuitive mode of thinking, the accessing of multiple probabilities, you can then begin to direct your intuition purposely toward specific probabilities you wish to manifest. Your paintings will reflect that purpose through the designs that manifest from your intuition. Your intuitive thinking will translate the probability into a symbol, charged with the energy of your intent and creative will. And these probabilities can mesh with each other, as I find happens with my paintings. The painting becomes symbols upon symbols, encoded with meaning, intent, and desire. The paintings allow me access to those points of time I accessed in my intuitive state of mind.

A lot of what I've discussed in this chapter is similar to that on writing. Art is a different medium from writing, but nonetheless we have within art a way of shaping reality. It's no surprise that some societies try to censor and control the production of art and writing. Both forms of expression are ultimately uncontrollable, precisely because they take us to different points of space/time, opening us up to probability and imagination.

The points I've made in this chapter are, I believe, applicable to other forms of art than painting. Painting is the medium I know, but a sculptor could also apply the ideas to his/her magical workings. Likewise, any other artistic medium allows for this. The idea of the artistic process is that it taps us into a part of the self, an altered state of consciousness that we otherwise don't access in everyday life. Using that altered state of mind, the non-linear reality that is accessed, allow yourself actually to explore the probabilities of your life, using your art as the medium of your expression.

Exercises

1. If you never have worked with an artistic medium, start now. Try your hand at drawing, sculpting, painting, whatever appeals to you. Also, although classes are useful, you don't necessarily need to take classes to be an artist. I've never taken a painting course in my life, but for my purposes, my paintings work for me.

2. If you already practice a form of art, after an art session write down your impressions of your frame of mind. Were you in an intuitive state of mind when you did the art? If you weren't in an intuitive state, can you identify why you weren't? If you were in an intuitive state of mind, do you find yourself thinking of different probabilities while doing artwork? Don't worry if you don't, but next time you do artwork, let your mind wander.

Chapter Seven:
Space/Time Magic and Music

Although I'm not a musician, the making of music has always fascinated me. Once, when I lived in State College, Pennsylvania, I had the rare fortune of being allowed to sit in on a jam session by some of my musician friends. I say rare, because they didn't allow just anyone to sit in, and I soon realized why. The jam session produced some excellent music, but a large part of that was the dynamic of energy for the people doing the music. That dynamic was so powerful that a vortex of energy spun in the circle of the room, and I felt my consciousness drawn into it. Not only that, but I felt as if my face was literally changing shape. All of the musicians there also saw my face changing shape while they were playing. All of us were stunned, not sure what to make of what had happened, but I knew it was a special experience I'd been given, and it helped me realize that music shapes and changes the consciousness of the listener and the player.

Of course I'm not the only person to note this phenomenon. Music not only shapes the consciousness, but can also affect other aspects of human physiology. The concept of infrasound, for example, is a form of sound weaponry that can induce sickness and death, and has been around since the sixties: "In 1960 Professor Gavreau, head of the Electro-Acoustics and Automation Laboratory in France investigated the use of infrasonics as a weapon for military purposes. He devised a siren which emitted a note of 37 cycles, the effects of which could kill instantaneously when amplified to extremely high levels" (TAGC-Psychophysicist liner notes). Consider the music that you can listen to on the radio or on a tape/CD. There is some music that will make you happy, and other music that will make you sad. This doesn't happen just because of an emotional reaction. There are physiological reactions to sound, and these reactions trigger a change in consciousness and possibly health. Sound, after all, is vibration, and at the most fundamental level we are made up of specific vibrations, sound if you will, or so contemporary physicists suggest:

> According to string theory, the elementary ingredients of the universe are *not* point particles. Rather, they are tiny, one-dimensional filaments somewhat like infinitely thin rubber bands, vibrating to and fro. But don't let the name fool you: Unlike an ordinary piece of string, which is itself composed of molecules and atoms, the strings of string theory are purported to lie deeply within the heart of matter. The theory proposes that *they* are ultramicroscopic ingredients making up the particles out of which atoms themselves are made [Italics are the author's]."
>
> (The Elegant Universe- 1999, *Brian Greene*, p 136)

Disrupt the vibration and everything falls apart. But there are also ways of healing with sound, such as with healers who use the sounds of resonating crystal bowls as a means of attuning a person's energy, or vibration, as the case seems to be.

Play some music and listen to it. What are you really listening to? Are you listening to the vocals, or the beats, the vibrations? How do the vibrations, the beats, make you feel? Incidentally, I'm not dismissing the importance of vocals in music. I find, however, more often than not, that the vocals act as a distraction, so for myself, I usually play "soundscapes" for ritual magic. I do any vocalization myself, or another person directly involved in the ritual will do it. For you, vocals might be useful. Experiment and explore with music that works best for you in ritual.

What's really intriguing is that while modern physics is just coming around to this way of understanding sound and its relationship to our essential state of existence, other cultures have long acknowledged the role of sound and vibration in the universe:

For thousands of years the sacred texts of India have taught that sound holds the key to the universe, to the creation and sustaining of our world, and to the means of extricating ourselves from its bonds. In the Eastern tradition the world of phenomenon is seen as a reflection of the infinite combinations of sound patterns, all derived from the soundless sound of the one who creates.

(TAGC-Psychophysicist liner notes)

Not too surprisingly, several magic systems from the Far East employ sound as a way of creating a different state of mind, and even of body. For instance, in Tibet, the utterance of certain combinations of sounds can produce different effects: "After *Hik!* he shouts *phat!* But he must be careful not to articulate *phat* when he is only practicing, like the monks you overheard. The combination of those two sounds invariably leads to the separation of body and spirit, so that the lama who pronounced them correctly over himself would immediately die" (Magic and Mystery in Tibet – 1971, *Alexandra David-Neel,* p. 14). The combination of sounds produces an effect, and that effect would seem physiological if it induces death. But sound needn't be used solely to induce death. It can also induce visions, as David-Neel noted happened for some participants in another ritual she observed (1988). Brennan notes:

Both Bon and Buddhist monasteries make considerable use of sound as part of their spiritual practice. Virtually every surviving temple has its own 'orchestra,' but the work of that orchestra seems to be something other than the production of music as it is known in the West. Its function is to create specific combinations of sounds as an aid to activities like meditation.

(Occult Tibet – 2002, *J. H. Brennan,* p. 34)

Beyond the Tibetan approaches to sound there is also, in Tantra, the use of mantras, words vocalized as a way of getting in touch with the vibrational energy the words represent. Vocalization is the vibration of a word or syllable, deep in your throat. As an experiment, put your fingers on your throat and say a word. Notice how your throat vibrates just a little bit. That's your vocal cords at work. Now vocalize the word. Say the sound from deeper in your throat and again put your fingers on your throat. You'll feel more of a vibration, more power in the utterance.

The use of sound, of vocalization and vibration, is not limited to Far Eastern systems of belief. The Qabala, which includes the "names of God," uses the Middle Pillar exercise as a way of protecting the person, through the vocalization of the names. Each name represents a different energy, and all of these energies are activated through sound. In other Western approaches to magic, sound can be instrumental in performing specific magical techniques. William G. Gray acknowledges the power of sound in invocation magic:

> Beings that live beyond the boundaries of physical matter will only 'hear' us if we address them with Inner sonics uttered through our own Inwardising consciousness. In other words, the Gods hear us in ourselves – if we are effectively connected to Them by Inner channels. During ritual working, sonics are usually divided between utterers and listeners...The job of the utterer, is to aim sonically at whatever Inner contact is sought via the hearers, whose function it is to link themselves with that particular contact and no other...It means that while a skilled Invocant is emitting meaningful sonic energies directed to some category of the Universal Consciousness, those hearing them physically are acting as receptive relays sending the message backwards through themselves, along their inner linkage with the Contact they are all trying to reach.
>
> (Magical Ritual Methods – 1969, *William G. Gray,* p. 176-177)

Sound acts as the medium of expression, the transferal of energy, and the connection of the god force to the invocants. And much of this sound is directed inward, vibrated in the throat, as opposed to being merely spoken through the mouth. Sound is acknowledged as a power that has an effect on the consciousness of those involved in the ritual. I invite you to read William G. Gray's works further for more on his fascinating approaches to sound and magic in general.

Music and magic have a rich history of involvement with each other. And when you add space/time workings into the mix, it can only get more fascinating. The first aspect to explore is the music that specifically deals with space/time workings. Or, if it's your fancy, creating music that focuses on specific kinds of workings can also be useful. The music should evoke a sense of difference from what you normally hear: "Having music in 'weird' tunings separates it from the music you usually hear and adds to its potency in healing and trance work" (Acoustic Signals – 2004, *Greg Turner,* p. 37). I find that for space/time workings that involve music I usually aim for trance, although using music for healing is also equally important, and can be useful for space/time workings, depending on what you seek to heal. It is also important to reserve the music you want to use for space/time workings just for those actual workings. If you listen to the music all the time, it might not have the same effect on you as it would if you kept it for solely for occasions when you've created a definite intention to perform space/time magic.

To understand this further, let's consider what music can do to your physiology. The sound of music operates on frequencies, and specific frequencies will trigger neurological changes in the transmitters of the brain:

> Each brain center generates impulses at a certain frequency based on the predominant neurotransmitters it secretes, in other words, the brains internal communication system (the language) is based on frequencies. Presumably, when we send waves of external energy at, say, 10hz, certain cells in the lower brain stem will respond because they normally fire within that particular frequency range; as a result, specific mood-altering chemicals associated with that region will be released.
>
> (TAGC Teste Tones liner notes)

As you can see it's literally possible to get high off music. The electrochemicals that are stimulated help to create an altered state of mind. This is why with some types of music, particularly trance, electronica, and industrial (but also other types), people will get high when listening to it. I like using this kind of music for my rituals, because it helps with the creation of environment. If you think about it, the high frequencies of the music lend themselves to the energy that you intend to work with. And not only does the music contribute toward creating an altered sacred consciousness, it has therapeutic effects as well: "They [high frequency sounds] work directly on the cortex of the brain; it mobilizes the complimentary forces of the human system and provides a natural high and a natural sedative, consequently counteracting against audiogenic attack, which we all undergo during the course of a normal days exposure to low frequency vibration-due to industrial processes and motor vehicle noises, etc." (TAGC Teste Tone Liner Notes). The types of music you listen to can create altered states of consciousness, and for the purposes of space/time magic this altered state of consciousness can lead to access of other probabilities of which you might otherwise be unaware.

When I use music in space/time magical workings, I pick very specific music. I'll list below some of the bands that I've found useful for this kind of work, and mention several specific albums. I generally use the music either for trance work or a specific ritual. Naturally, this music lends itself to all kinds of rituals besides space/time magic, but mostly I listen to certain music in order to trance out, and use my altered state of conscious to explore non-linear reality, either through examining multiple probabilities or reliving a specific moment of my past as present. Using this kind of music for rituals helps create an atmosphere that feels otherworldly and open to different versions of reality.

There are a number of musicians whose work I recommend using for magical rituals. Some of my recommendations aren't necessarily for rituals, however, and in those cases I'll differentiate.

The first group I recommend is Current 93, specifically the white noise albums such as "Dog's Blood Rising," or even the double CD compilation "In Menstrual Blood." White noise is music that involves the recording of noises of everyday life and then filtering them into music with beats and sound. Current 93's later compositions – apocalyptic folk music – are really good, but don't work for me for the purposes of magical workings. Nurses with Wound, a spin off band from Current 93, has more white noise music.

Another group I highly recommend is Coil. The album I like to use for space/time magic is "Timemachines." That particular album, through music, duplicates the effects of specific drugs on the neurotransmitters by isolating the frequencies that those drugs create when stimulating the neurotransmitters. Another Coil album I like is the "Zos/Kia Live" album. I played that during my last death-rebirth ritual (for details on the ritual, read Appendix A).

Finally, a musical group I have actually cited in this chapter, The Anti-Group Collective, makes music for the express purposes of experimenting with how it affects the neurotransmitters. Any of their albums will be sufficient for experimenting with how music can alter the consciousness of the mind, and you can find information about those albums in the bibliography of this book. Other musicians you may wish to look into are Rapoon, Dead Voices on Air, Scorn, Steve Roach, Not Breathing, and The Swans. I'm certain that my recommendations haven't even begun to cover all of the groups and musicians who, in one form or another, produce music that can put you into an altered state of mind.

As you can see by now, music has a powerful effect on our physiology. While I haven't made specific references to space/time magic and music, I hope I have made it clear how music can be used in magical workings, including space/time magic. In order to understand how to use it, you first have to understand what a tool does. In this case, we know that music has an effect on us, that cultures have recognized the power of sound and vibration as not merely a way of altering the physiology of a person, but also of reality itself. Awareness of this can lead you to experiment with different musical groups, but also with sound itself, exploring how the use of vibration and vocalization can create altered states of mind, as well as techniques that can be used for other practical forms of magic, be it invocation, healing, evocation, or something else.

For instance, I find that vocalizing a specific word or syllable can be very useful during visualizations. When I use Reiki energy to heal people, I trace the symbols and vocalize them, summoning the energy through both the sound of my voice and the gestures I use to emphasize that sound. Likewise, with some Tibetan meditations, the vocalization of a syllable is part of how the energy is raised. The sound of the syllable is used to raise the vibrations of a person's energy. This applies to space/time magic in that I sometimes use the vocalization to invoke the forces that I associate and work with for space/time magic. The vocals help to establish the environment that I feel lends itself to space/time workings and the access of probabilities.

To use the Reiki example again, in relationship to space/time magic, what I do with the sound is vocalization. I charge the words with vibrations, as I utter the words low in my throat. As I do this, I visualize the Reiki energy permeating every cell, every atom, every particle of my body, but at the same time I extend this visualization outward. I visualize every possibility that I can imagine in the universe being filled with Reiki energy. I do this every day, and I find it useful for helping me to achieve a state of mind where I can tune into the vibrational patterns of the universe.

Simply put, sound is a powerful medium of magic. Those of you who have an opportunity should consider how to use sound in your magical workings. You'll inevitably find, as I have, that sound lends itself to creating the altered realities we seek to manifest. We connect with the vibrations of the universe and we tune those vibrations to our needs, to the manifestation we seek to realize concretely in our everyday lives.

In several of the upcoming chapters, I'll explore further how sound is used in space/time workings, specifically with technology and meditation.

Exercises

112

1. Familiarize yourself with a culture that uses sound in one form or another to do magic. I recommend Tibetan magic. Once you've familiarized yourself with how sound is used, experiment with it. Vocalize and vibrate some of the syllables. Record how this makes you feel.

2. If possible, check out one of the music recommendations I've made. Listen to the album without doing a ritual, and after it has finished write down how it made you feel while you were listening to it. Did you feel any different from how you did before? If so, how?

Chapter Eight:
Space/Time Magic and Science

A book on space/time magic would hardly be complete without a look at science, and how it can be integrated into space/time workings. As I mentioned in the first chapter, many people conceive space/time as being linear, with one event leading to another. However, as science has advanced, so, too, has its understanding of what space/time is, and how it works. And while relativity theory continues to espouse a linear, causal reality of space/time, such is not the case with quantum theory. It is this theory of space/time that interests me, because it best explains the existence of magic and how it can even exist in the first place. Carroll explains quantum theory in the following passage:

> In quantum theory any further subdivision beyond the quantization level is achieved by probabilistic distribution of the particle itself. Thus in the quantum description a particle can be instantaneously everywhere although most of its existence is mainly concentrated on one small place in space-time. Quantum theory describes a universe based not on causality and determinism, but on probability and indeterminism, in which processes are discontinuous and instantaneous signals can be exchanged.
> (Liber Kaos -1992, *Peter Carroll,* p. 5)

As can be seen, a quantum model of science easily explains magic and the various results associated with it. A quantum model also explains retroactive magic, because if the probability is instantaneously everywhere, it also exists every *when,* and thus can become manifested as reality, regardless of the linear stage of reality. Certainly, if nothing else, the quantum theory agrees with the concept that perception shapes reality, and that pattern and picture appear, even if nothing is there.

Consider, for instance, the constellations. Objectively, all we really see is a collection of stars in the sky, but subjectively we create meaning and shape out of them, shaping reality as we do so into what we want it to be, as opposed to what "objectively" exists, and this applies as well to everyday life: "It has been shown experimentally through the viewing of random white dots on a screen that man tends to find pattern and picture where objectively there is none: his mental processes shapes what it sees" (The Job – 1969, *Daniel Odier,* p. 173). Now, if this occurs in everyday life – and it seems to – what happens at the quantum level? What seems to occur is that when the quantum level is examined, our perceptions of what we see shape the possibilities that are represented at this level. This means that, despite the seemingly linear nature of reality, we really exist in a state of probability, where the nature of reality is malleable.

At this point you might be wondering, if reality is so malleable, why is it also so uniform? There are several factors that can be used to explain this. Reality is not as uniform or consensual as we believe it to be. You only need to go to a different culture to get a different understanding of reality, and in fact you can make it even more simplistic than that. Talk to the person next to you and invariably you'll find that person disagrees with you on some subject. How does that make reality different? The person next you to mediates reality differently than you do. You may both agree that grass is green, but s/he may feel that the current president is excellent while you do not, or you might both disagree on the grass's shade of green. And while that is just a matter of perception, it nonetheless shows that people do not always live in the same reality tunnel as everyone else.

Reality is also malleable in terms of probability, and specifically the awareness that each person cultivates in regards to probability. Why is it that some people have more possibilities than others? Undoubtedly, the argument will come up that an individual's socioeconomic status affects the probabilities that s/he is aware of, but I don't think we can reduce awareness of possibilities to just that category. There have been many people who started out poor in life and ended up much better off. They did this by cultivating awareness of possibility, looking for the opportunities they could use to elevate their lifestyles. Those who make themselves self aware of possibilities and are willing to be creative in how they live their lives will find more opportunities than people who allow themselves to be limited into uniformity.

Schooling is another factor in the apparent uniformity of society. Schooling is often used as a way of imprinting norms that the majority of society embraces. So, for instance, if you think stealing isn't socially acceptable, but everyone else is taught that it is acceptable, chances are that to due to social pressure you'll end up agreeing that stealing is socially acceptable and should be done.

Historically and socially, the magician is a person on the fringe of society, a person with a different perception and awareness from the majority. Accordingly, that different perception allows for more opportunities than the average person is aware of. However, we can take this argument in another direction.

Usually in high school you will find groups of people considered popular and groups or individuals who are considered to be "geeks" or "different." It's intriguing to note that the majority of truly successful people are those who were once considered geeks, or undesirably different, because they didn't conform to a specific code of behavior. The popular kids usually end up in mainstream society, holding jobs that the majority of people hold. They do not have the same perspective or grasp of possibility possessed by someone who has been kept on the fringe. It's a difference in perspective, and although reality seems to conform to a uniform, consensual perspective of it, in fact it does not, when it is examined at the individual level.

Environment is another factor. Depending on where you are raised, you will have a different understanding of reality from

117

people from another region. For instance, inner city school kids who get to go out to a farm are usually filled with wonder and surprise at a reality they've never experienced, and vice versa for a child who lives in the country. An inner city kid in his/her environment will have much more awareness of possibilities in that environment, as opposed to a farm where s/he needs to learn more about the environment before finding out about the possibilities within it.

How all of this applies to science is that science suggests that reality is malleable, that we can shape it through our perceptions, and more specifically our awareness of probability, by being aware of the subtle nature of reality. As an example, consider special relativity: "Special relativity, however, proclaims that the differences in observations between two such individuals are more subtle and profound. It makes the strange claim that observers in relative motion will have different perceptions of distance and time" (The Elegant Universe – 1999, *Brian Greene,* p. 25). Those differing perceptions will be accurate for both people, for the simple fact that the reality that they experienced was shaped by their perceptions. One aspect of science that is often ignored is that it is the attempt to explain the nature of reality. And yet the different perceptions that we have shape our understanding of science, which is why there is still no universal theory to explain why the universe is the way it seems to be. Instead, science provides different paradigms of reality. There's no guarantee that any of these paradigms is accurate, but they can be useful for the magician to use in the melding of scientific thought to magical action.

The paradigm of science I use in magical workings is that of I.T. or Imaginary Time. Stephen Hawking came up with the term and concept, but both magicians and scientists use it to this day. We can understand I.T. in the following sense:

> Imaginary time sounds like something from science fiction, but it is a well-defined mathematical concept: time measured in what are called imaginary numbers. One can think of ordinary real numbers such as 1, 2, -3.5, and so on as corresponding to positions on a line stretching from left to

right: zero in the middle, positive real numbers on the right, and negative real numbers on the left. Imaginary numbers can then be represented as corresponding to positions on a vertical line: zero is again in the middle, positive imaginary numbers plotted upward, and negative imaginary numbers plotted downward.

(The Universe in a Nutshell - 2001, *Stephen Hawking,* p. 59)

Using both the real numbers and the imaginary numbers, you can plot out probabilities, determining how much effort is needed to manifest the probability into reality. In other words, in science, imaginary time explains how you can have such a probability laden universe. And this definition isn't limited to one universe. Rather, I.T. also allows for the exploration of parallel universes. These realities exist, both horizontally and vertically to your own reality. You can use it, and specifically the real and imaginary numbers, not just as ways of charting probabilities, but also of charting other realities. You can create or perceive patterns in I.T. that allow you to manipulate the probabilities into reality. You simply have to be aware that there are multiple potential realities, and each of these potentialities is accessible through understanding how they intersect with each other. If you don't like Hawking's model, you can think of I.T. along the lines of the Shamanic understanding of the universe, namely, the web of power. Each point on the web of power represents a probability, and the strands that connect the points to each other represent the relationship of each probability to another. Whenever you manifest one probability, you change the pattern of the web, the relationship of the web to yourself and your reality. But to do this effectively, it is essential to understand the pattern of the web, the way probabilities connect to and affect each other. You need to understand how the "past" and the "future" probabilities affect each other, return to each other, and form the pattern out of each other. In other words, the past and future aren't static concepts, but rather interactive forces that interface with each other to form the pattern of the web that you or I call the present. Naturally, to work knowingly with these probabilities requires some visualization and other techniques.

119

A magical perspective on I.T. offers its own theories and practices. Peter Carroll offers this view of imaginary time:

> On the other hand, shadow or imaginary time accords much better with the idea of an indeterminate future containing many possible alternatives, or parallel universes. It also implies a multitude of possible pasts, despite the fact that most people seem to suffer from only a single past in their memories. We remember only the real-time past, which was singular at the moment it occurred; after it has occurred, all pasts, which could have given rise to the new moment of the real-time present, will exist in imaginary time, while the real-time past has of course ceased to exist.
>
> (Liber Kaos -1992, *Peter Carroll*, p. 35)

Imaginary time, from this perspective, allows for retroactive magic. Although we seem to have one defined, set past, in fact, through I.T., we can access multiple pasts, multiple probabilities that affect the present in which we live. This also applies to the future. You need to understand how to access more than what is on the surface, in this case, the surface being the concept that time is an unbroken line with one past and one future.

Another perspective on I.T. is Genesis P-orridge's approach to it. A brief disclaimer: some of the spellings in this essay by him are based on TOPY's (Temple of Psychic Youth's) changes to the English language. They use phonetic spellings, so as to alter the consciousness of the reader by forcing him/her to focus on the words. For Genesis, a synthesis of space/time magic involves not merely I.T., but also concepts such as DNA: "Everything we assemble becomes, and is, a description ov what we are now or what we 'being' at any level; from thee deepest, sub-molecular, neurodimensional reaches that we have named 'DNA' to thee farthest interdimensional reaches ov galactic expansions and contractions outside TIME or SPACE" (Rebels & Devils: The Psychology of Liberation - 1996, *Genesis P-orridge*, p. 336). Of course, by going beyond time and space, we supplant it, master it, and consequently move past the need for it. But is that necessarily what Genesis is really doing? Can we even get beyond space and time?

I think we can alter our understanding of space and time, interact with it in different ways and BREAK the definitions of space/time that have been imprinted upon us by a society that prefers to manacle us with watches that keep us on schedule and stressed out. Contemporary American society has a clock in every room, on every computer, silently ticking away the space/time you have to exist. Being put on a schedule like that can ultimately be frustrating, if only because it seems that we are caught in the ominous linear inevitability of time. But, as I've maintained throughout this book, such a linear perspective is ultimately flawed, and we can move outside it, outside space/time as we are taught to think of it.

For Genesis this involves a technique called splintering, a technique similar to the collage/cut-ups of Burroughs and Gysin. It allows for getting outside space/time:

> We are choosing SPLINTERS consciously and unconsciously to represent our own memetic (DNA) patterns, our own cultural imprints and aspirations. We are in a truly Magickal sense 'INVOKING' manifestations, perhaps even results, in order to confound and short-circuit our perceptions, and reliance upon 'WHOLENESS'. We are creating our own subjective and speculative descriptions ov 'OTHERNESS'
> (Rebels & Devils: The Psychology of Liberation – 1996, *Genesis P-orridge*, p. 336)

But even if you have a sense of how to get outside space/time, to splinter the perceptions of wholeness and create otherness, you nonetheless need a concrete technique to make this work for you. Genesis's approach is more artistic than scientific, at least by the perspective of the science community. He takes apart image, noise, and other forms of space/time, and reassembles them into something else, a transmutation of space/time into otherness, a splintering of reality into multiple realities. But I think there is a science at work, albeit a science that involves an awareness of how to separate our linear reality through sound, image, and other sensory means. Are you trapped by your senses? Or do you change your perspective, make it your own, and consequentially every moment you have experienced and will experience, by willfully making it more than what linear reality dictates it can be? The science, in this case, is based on symbols, altering meaning, infusing desire, and shaping reality, but nonetheless also involves understanding how the manipulation of media has an affect on the human psyche. You've been conditioned for so long to live in a linear reality, to live by logic, that you've come to rely less upon your intuition, upon a non-linear recognition of reality, a flowing and bending with reality, as opposed to a dictation by an elite few of what reality should be. And while logic has its place and usefulness, balancing it with your intuition, learning to take a non-linear approach to reality, can only benefit you, making you more aware of possibility, opening your perspectives up, and allowing you to seize opportunities not readily apparent, by simply not accepting the monotonous, ominous tone of linear reality ringing from the bells of a church.

But where does Genesis's approach to I.T. fit into all of this? For P-orridge, I.T. is not necessarily what Hawking or Carroll is speaking of, but something entirely different:

> This activation ov popular culture, or Transmedia exploration as we would designate I.T. (where I.T.= Imaginary TIME), E would argue, is parallel to an All-Chemical phenomenon. There is knowing and precise refining ov 'matter', its origin being at this stage in Astory, any information in any medium ever recorded in any possible or impossible process whatsoever.
>
> (Rebels & Devils: The Psychology of Liberation – 1996,
> *Genesis P-orridge*, p. 338)

So I.T. is not just parallel universes rife with probability, but is also in everything that has been created or otherwise used as a means of transmitting information. And in its own way, this definition makes sense. Consider, for instance, that it's much harder to make an informed decision about a matter of concern without having information. But information in any form won't necessarily do either. A refinement of the information, a narrowing down of the relevant information, is necessary for maximum probability. Quite simply, this is because, as with anything else, too much information will only end up confusing the probabilities. To effectively manipulate I.T. involves discerning the relevant information and using it accordingly, remaking it, changing it to access the probabilities that are required to make a choice, or multiple choices. This remaking can involve some artistic splintering/collage work, but it can also go beyond that. What I find useful in this approach is not merely doing the splinter test, but becoming the splintering, splintering myself, accessing all potential probabilities, and living them out through my intuitive understanding of them.

You can remake yourself into I.T. It simply involves changing your perspective, cultivating as many different approaches to the subject, to the choices, as possible. But, you might say, there's never enough time. If this is your response, quit being defined by time, by the tick of the clock, the limitations of definition. Change reality by understanding that you can define it just as any other person can: "We are thee source ov all that we invoke. What we define and describe exists through our choosing to describe I.T. By continued and repeated description ov its parameters and nature, we animate I.T. We give I.T. life" (Rebels & Devils: The Psychology of Liberation – 1996, *Genesis P-orridge*, p. 345). In other words, the choices you make are the choices you create, invoke, and evoke. It's not merely, after all, that you bring those choices inward, but that you also manifest them outward into dynamic reality. I.T. then is the process of accessing, making and creating choices where seemingly none existed. The cultivation of perception, of awareness of more than linear time, is essential for accessing I.T.

Another paradigm or scientific approach to space/time magic is the holographic model. This model, while in some ways similar to I.T. (namely through the access of multiple probabilities), takes a different approach to space/time, arguing that all the probabilities of space/time are holographically available, as opposed to becoming accessible through I.T. by the manipulation and awareness of probability in reality. Nonetheless, as a paradigm, the holographic universe can be extremely useful to the magician. Nor does the holographic model rule out parallel realities; thus the enterprising magician can easily use a synthesis of I.T. and the holographic model.

Still, in order to understand the holographic paradigm and space/time, it's instructive to consider how this paradigm approaches the subject: "Our brains mathematically construct objective reality by interpreting frequencies that are ultimately projections from another dimension, a deeper order of existence that is beyond both space and time: The brain is a hologram enfolded in a holographic universe" (The Holographic Universe – 1991, *Michael Talbot,* p. 54). One problem with this approach is the claim of an objective universe constructed by mathematics. The reason this claim is faulty is that mathematics is ultimately another form/descriptor language. It's a language imposed on reality in an attempt to understand reality, but it never captures the complete picture. Also, the very act of interpretation draws upon the subjectivity of the person doing the interpreting. All of us tend to interpret reality in terms of the subjective reality tunnel we inhabit. This isn't to say this definition can't work, but even making it work seems to require that you bring it into your subjective understanding of the definition. If nothing else, remember that when you work with space/time magic, or any magic, or any approach to life, inevitably you will still regard them from a subjective viewpoint. You can and should be aware of your subjective nature, but you shouldn't buy into the deluded concept of an entirely objective universe, because the very act of experience means that you interpret and mediate the situation into your own subjective understanding of it and the probabilities it makes you aware of. This isn't to say that events don't occur separate from you, or that people don't exist separate from you, but once you encounter those events and people, you mediate them into your own versions or reality. Just as other people do with you.

However, the holographic paradigm is still useful for the magician to employ in space/time workings. For instance, the holographic approach to space/time magic argues that synchronicities, which are events that happen in conjunction with each other, despite appearing to be random, are a product of the mesh of our inner psychological state of mind with reality around us: "Peat thinks that synchronicities reveal the absence of division between the physical world and our inner psychological reality. Thus the relative scarcity of synchronous experiences in our lives shows not only the extent to which we have fragmented ourselves from the general field of consciousness, but also the degree potential of the deeper orders of the mind" (The Holographic Universe – 1991, *Michael Talbot,* p. 80). The idea that the inner state of mind mirrors the outer state of reality falls into line with the occult principle of: as above, so below. What occurs in the mind has an effect on the environment around you, even as the environment around you has an effect on your mental processes. Synchronicity, which is really the alignment of probability, occurs most often when you know yourself thoroughly and can imprint that knowing into the reality around you. In other words, when you are in touch with yourself, you are also in touch with the probabilities that favor you the most. For instance, as a writer I can readily attest to the amount of synchronicities related to my writing that have occurred in the last two years. But many of those occurrences happened because I contacted particular people or looked into a particular event. Sometimes friends helped me out. The synchronicities resulted because I infused purpose into manifesting a particular reality.

Still, not all synchronicities will seem favorable to someone when they occur. In February 2004, I did a death/rebirth ritual (full details can be found in Appendix A) to gain some perspective in my life. I didn't realize that the ritual would end up taking a lot longer than I expected. To explain that, I should say that the actual ritual only took several days, but the synchronicities from that ritual haven't stopped manifesting even now. At times, I felt that the synchronicities that did occur were the worst possible probabilities that could happen. I didn't realize at the time that what seemed bad to me would end up ultimately being beneficial, with me gaining far more from the attendant synchronicities than I originally thought.

The holographic paradigm also focuses on space/time magic in regards to retroactive magic: "Bohm's notion that the flow of time is the product of a constant series of unfoldings and enfoldings suggests that as the present enfolds and becomes part of the past, it does not cease to exist, but simply returns to the cosmic storehouse of the implicate" (The Holographic Universe – 1991, *Michael Talbot,* p. 200). If the past returns to a storehouse of sorts, it's still accessible. Our memories are proof of that, because we do access the past through them. In the holographic paradigm, every moment of time exists in and of itself and can be accessed, because that moment never ceases to be. The moment is always there. It is just our memories that are faulty. Similarly, the concept of precognition is one that the holographic paradigm explores. The holographic paradigm argues that the future is predetermined, but that there are parallel futures: "The future of any given holographic universe *is* predetermined, and when a person has a precognitive glimpse of the future they are tuning into the future of that particular hologram only. But like amoebas, these holograms also occasionally swallow and engulf each other, melding and bifurcating like the protoplasmic globs of energy that they really are" (The Holographic Universe – 1991, *Michael Talbot,* p. 211). So for the holographic paradigm, a precognition is really a *recognition* of a set future. To get out of that future, you need to move from one hologram to another. In other words, you need to shift from one parallel universe to another.

While the holographic paradigm has its uses, it seems too limiting to me. The idea of a predetermined future rules out probability. And if the only way to get to a probability is to shift from one reality to another, to change holograms, it still seems like you or I could be limiting ourselves. But again, as with any other model, the holographic paradigm is not the territory. It's just a map. If it works for you, use it. Or, if you're like me, take what does work from that model and discard the rest.

The final magical/scientific model I want to explore is Stephen Mace's approach to space/time magic. Mace is a useful resource for working probability magic, specifically because he does apply a scientific mindset to how magic works. Many magicians approach magic with the idea that it doesn't matter how it works so long as it does work. But this kind of thinking is flawed. Not knowing how something works is like holding a metal rod up to the sky while lightning is striking. You might get lucky and not get hit by lightning, but chances are you will get hit. Similarly, if you don't know how the magic works, or why something occurs, and just write it off as acausal, without understanding the why of it, you are displaying a sign of an undisciplined approach to magic. And when you need the magic to work, it might not work, and then what will you do? While you might never have all the answers or explanations for why something happened, it's important to at least formulate an idea. Plus by knowing how the magic works, why something occurs, you'll know when to use the magic and how to get the most out of using it when the situation is right.

Mace's paradigm resolves to explain why manifestation of probability occurs:

> I would suggest that 'occult' or 'acausal' manifestations like omens and the results of successful conjurations occur due to a filling of latent forms, unseen patterns that lie at the roots of our world, yet which never show themselves and so must be inferred if they are to be manipulated. These forms operate without physical reference to physical bodies or events. Rather, they give shape to the bodies and events, and make possible both the fantastic diversity and the innate unity of the physical universe.
> (Sorcery as Virtual Mechanics – 1999, *Stephen Mace.* p. 4)

In other words, magic occurs because we access these patterns and from them produce manifestation. Likewise, synchronicity is a manipulation of these patterns. If you approach magic in this manner, consider that the rituals we do are a means of giving these unseen patterns shape. The rituals we do create the distinct probability we want to manifest into reality. That probability is imposed upon the patterns, and if enough energy is put into the probability it manifests, changing the patterns as a result. This also occurs with synchronicities, but not through a directed medium such as ritual. It's undirected and unconscious for you, but only for the simple fact that the tension in your life needs an outlet, and accordingly sends signals (synchronicity) to you, to let you know that a change is needed.

The way to achieve a purposeful manipulation of synchronicity is to use techniques that don't directly involve you, but allow for the alignment of probability into reality through the manipulation of energy: "The act of conjuring manufactures the tension that fills the form the conjurer defines 'above,' spawning the beneficial event 'below.' The particular problems of conjuring involves the definition of an efficacious virtual form, the production of sufficient energy to actualize it, and the focusing of the energy into the form so it does actually fill it, rather than in any way misfiring" (Sorcery as Virtual Mechanics – 1999, *Stephen Mace*. p. 10). Mace further equates form with quantum physics in the following definition: "The unfulfilled forms of particles, forms whose existence physicists infer because if they supply free energy, 'actual,' detectable particles come into existence" (Sorcery as Virtual Mechanics – 1999, *Stephen Mace*. p. 17). On a quantum level, physics duplicates what the sorcerer does, in that the sorcerer utilizes energy to create a form by which you can actualize the desire you seek to manifest, and likewise the physicist, by providing energy, creates the particles s/he desires to perceive.

Of course, magic works because you are able to impose your version of reality upon the so-called objective reality around you. Your mind gives form to the energy, and then the energy is applied to the patterns of reality to produce a new reality, a manifestation that favors you, although you also need to cover any other bases in the manifestation of probability into reality: "Rather than finding out what's true or what's false, those who work to manipulate energy on a quantum level do so by conforming to a convention, creating a middle ground occupied both by themselves and the unknowable quantum stuff" (Sorcery as Virtual Mechanics – 1999, *Stephen Mace*. p. 12). That middle ground involves you doing more than just creating the ritual and firing off the intention. Creating the middle ground means you create the physical circumstances for the quantum energy to manifest the probability into reality. For instance, if you want a job, a sigil to get a job will do no good, unless you actually go and fill out applications. This is what it means to create a middle ground in magical practice.

What I've presented in this chapter has not merely been a synthesis of magic and science, but also primarily the only approaches that have been taken with space/time magic. I've found that most people only associate science and magic as the means to work space/time magic. By now I hope that my previous chapters have disproved that notion. I feel strongly that if I do not cover the angle of science and magic in this book I'll leave out a critical area of study and practice in space/time magic. I can't say that I've covered every scientific approach in this chapter, but I have attempted to give you a sense of some of the paradigms in use by sorcerers like myself who employ a synthesis of science and magic in their workings.

My next chapter on meditation will actually employ some of what I mention here. It's fair to say the next chapter is my own approach to space/time magic. While I employ all of the techniques mentioned in this book to some degree, the following chapter will give you an idea of what I conceive space/time to be, and how I've worked with it.

Exercises

1. I've identified a few scientific paradigms in this chapter. Do some more research on these paradigms, or, alternatively, explore some other scientific approaches to space/time and see how you can synthesize a magical approach of the scientific principles.

2. You can also explore the mathematical approaches to space/time magic, if you wish. A good place to start, especially for those of you who like myself are mathematically inept, is with a textbook on abstract mathematics. I recommend *Discrete Mathematics* (publishing details may be found in the bibliography). By learning to approach math from an

abstract angle, you will find how it can be used for alternate solutions. It's also useful for making sense of some of the equations you'll find in the science books.

Chapter Nine:
Invocation, Evocation, and Meditation

For me, meditation has been the most useful way of working with space/time magic. This makes sense, given that in meditation I'm altering my mental state, accessing different levels of consciousness. Meditation has also allowed me to explore and develop my own paradigm of space/time magic.

The type of meditation I use is called Offnung. Offnung is a hermetic meditation that enables you to tap into the universal subconscious of the human collective mind. The magician acts as a reference point in Offnung, an open door, if you will. This can work exceedingly well with space/time magic, as it enables you not only to act as a beacon for other forces of magic, but also for yourself – that is, as a beacon to the different layers of consciousness you explore in the self. You can access yourself as a reference point at any point in the space/time continuum and simultaneously at multiple points of the space/time continuum. You become the axis mundi, the doorway to all probabilities.

When I refer to multiple points I mean the parallel universes along the DNA strand of the multiverse (this concept is explained later in this chapter), wherein exist the presence of multiple selves – multiple yous – as reference points. Consequently, being aware of yourself in this way means that you can be aware of the reference points of both yourself and others – specifically, how those reference points affect the fields of possibility you will manipulate to work magic. With this understanding, you can capitalize on yourself as multiple reference points in the multiverse, drawing not only on other powers, both within and without yourself, but also on the possibilities which affect you as a cosmic reference point.

As we act as reference points, we also act as a connection to other reference points and to the DNA of the multiverse. We are parts of the endless spiral, and through our understanding of the spiral, so too can we understand the nature of possibility through Offnung. Space/time magic is a realization of the multi-layered nature of our consciousness, and working with Offnung allows us to access those layers, so as to not only increase awareness of possibility, but also to increase the ability to manipulate possibility into reality.

I have modified the original Offnung meditation to better pursue space/time magic. The original version focuses on using pranayama (an Indian breathing technique, in which you breathe in through the nose and out through the mouth, with the goal being to raise your life energy through the act of breathing). My modification includes adding self-hypnosis to the visualization process of the pranayamic breathing. I've found that this addition makes the meditation very successful, and it has led me to intriguing places and concepts of being, including the oblivion of "myself." It helps me get deeper into the meditative trance.

First, I speak aloud, explaining to myself the goal of the meditation. Then, I say that the 100 breaths I will take are stairs to a door that will open to where I need to go. I also focus on relaxing my body, so that I feel a tingling soothing energy in my muscles. I tell myself that for the first ten breaths my feet will feel a tingly energy that will make the muscles relax. I then take a breath and count to ten out loud. I start the first ten breaths with my feet, the next ten with my calves, the next ten with my thighs, thirty-one through forty on my hands, forty-one through fifty on my forearms, fifty-one through sixty on my upper arms and shoulders. Sixty-one through seventy brings the tingling energy up from the hips to the shoulders. Seventy-one through eighty is focused on the neck, and eighty-one through ninety is focused on the head. The last ten breaths are used to get my entire body to slip deeper into the trance. When I reach the door at the hundredth breath I step through and start on my journey.

For people who might have trouble completing the count, record it on a tape recorder or have a friend speak the words and count for you. I do know that working Offnung with space/time is very powerful and very effective, as it taps you into the layers of consciousness within yourself that serve as cosmic reference points within the multiverse.

The original article on Offnung can be found online at:

http://misguided.darktech.org/~star/articles/alternthink.html

I first began working with the DNA spiral as a magical concept in 1998. The original working I did focused on identifying the five traditional elements of Western magic with the five DNA strands. A friend and I wanted to create a correspondence system with DNA and the elements. I also found the elemental workings to be a useful way to get to know the elements and how they are associated with the human body. Specifically, I created a ritual where I bonded the elements to my genetic struggle through the five strands of DNA. The idea was to create a resonance between the elemental energies and my own energy on a genetic level. We identified Uracil as Spirit or Ether, Adenine as Air, Guamine as Earth, Cytosine as Fire, and Thymine as Water. Although this was my initial working with DNA, I continued to develop my paradigm of DNA and magic as a way of not only doing elemental workings, but also for other purposes, including space/time magic.

The reason DNA works so well for space/time magic can be summed up as follows: "DNA symbolizes the fact that you are the universe in microcosm...The structure of DNA is such that any one part is like the whole. The micro reflects the macro. Similarly, each human being is both a part of the universe and a micro-expression of its totality" (Voyager Tarot – 1998, *James Wanless,* p. 13). As you can see, this concept of DNA, when applied to you, can become a doorway, much like the Offnung ritual. DNA serves as a useful paradigm to allow us to explore the probabilities inherent within and external to us.

I first got the idea to apply DNA to space/time magic through Warren Ellis's work on the *X-MAN* comic series. Ellis made the character of *X-MAN* into a shaman. This shaman would travel to a parallel version of Earth, and to do this he accessed a DNA spiral of probable Earths. He could travel up and down the spiral, though not sideways. Through meditation I can travel up and down the DNA spiral and sideways to another DNA spiral. Each element in the spiral represents a probable version of Earth, a probable reality that exists alongside our own probable reality. I can't travel there physically, but through the Offnung meditation I can still explore this model of the multiverse, and use it as a way both to understand and to shape probabilities.

One intriguing aspect of DNA is how it can be used to line up with the Qabalistic Tree of Life: "DNA, the crystal star flower, has ten points or petals. Ten symbolizes completion and represents the beginning of a new cycle that arises from the completion of an old one. Like the universe, you are whole in your cyclical, continuous progress of completion and beginning. DNA symbolizes the dynamic wholeness" (Voyager Tarot – 1998, *James Wanless,* p. 13-14). The Tree of Life has ten Sephiroth and these can be applied to the ten petals of the DNA flower of life. But there is another point here that relates to space/time magic. The DNA spiral I use in my workings is complete, but is always changing into a new cycle as choices are made and probabilities shift. Any point of the spiral is accessible, because the cycle, in being complete, has references to all probabilities, all choices. Another aspect of the DNA spiral is that, while it represents all probable versions of Earth, the paradigm is easy to shift. So, for instance, you can visualize that the DNA spiral represents all of your pasts and futures. Each point on the spiral represents a moment of the past that you may want to re-experience and change in some manner or form.

When I use this model for my meditations, I end up visualizing not just the planet Earth in a DNA spiral, but also all the other planets and stars. Also, I'll sometimes direct my consciousness to my Kundalini, and specifically to the tail of the serpent. For me, the tail is plunged into the Earth. It goes to the core of the planet, connecting me to its life force. And at the core of the Earth are lines of energy that vibrate from this planet to the other planets and the stars. These lines of energy connect the DNA spirals of the planets to each other, encoding the genetic information of the multiverse in the transmission of the connection. You can access that information, which is all the probabilities of space/time, and the DNA spirals, by traveling along those connections through your meditations. Again, I use the Offnung method of meditation for this kind of work. I'll let my consciousness sink into the Earth via the connection of the Kundalini Chakra. When I reach the core of the Earth, I extend my senses outward and find the lines of connection. I then travel along those lines to access the DNA spiral of probabilities for the Earth and the other planets and stars. I use this meditation to work with those DNA spirals and the patterns of energy that the connections between the planets and stars weave. This might sound a bit New Agey, but remember this is my model. It works for me. It might not work for you. You might want to adjust it, or change it around, or come up with a model of meditative space/time magic that works for you, and that's fine. My words are meant only to inspire. If you do find the DNA spiral meditation useful though, please do use it. I know for myself that it makes understanding the patterns of probabilities a bit easier, if only because I'm applying a paradigm that I'm familiar with to those patterns of probabilities.

Still, I haven't always used the DNA spiral for my space/time meditations. For a while I used the concept of Imaginary Time (I.T.). Again, I used the Offnung meditation, but I would visualize parallel realities. The more distant the probability, the more energy was required to access that reality and manifest it into my reality. I also find that using the math equations for I.T., particularly Peter Carroll's equations, can be a practice that aids in the meditation focused upon manifesting the probability. I usually take the answer and form it into a sigil, and use that sigil as the focus of my meditation, with the idea being that when I access the I.T. probability field I can gravitate toward the probability by the sigil I've used to represent it. The sigil acts as my beacon, and through it I can then not only access the probability, but also use the sigil to manifest that probability into reality, effectively changing the order of parallel universes by stepping out of one probable reality and into another. When I visualize probabilities in I.T., I often find myself before a gray void. Hovering in the void are bubbles, which are the probabilities. I can move to any of the bubbles, and when I touch the bubble I move into that probability.

One technique I've found useful for narrowing the field of probabilities in I.T., while at the same time gathering energy for a specific probability I wish to bring into reality, is what I call "popping the bubbles." First, I experience all the probabilities that I *don't* want to manifest. I do this so as to gradually become detached from them, and in that process take their energy. Once those undesired probabilities have no meaning or energy they cease to exist. I then apply the energy I've gained to a probability that I desire to manifest into this reality. I've found that using this technique makes manifesting the probability a lot easier. It also teaches you how to detach yourself from situations, people, etc., and that can be useful in the search for opportunity. You can likewise visualize yourself – and a future-self – as a bubble, with the future-self having some change about him/her or the events around him/her. Pop each bubble and let the energy of the "future you" mesh into the energy of the "present you," simultaneously focusing that energy on manifesting the change you want in your life.

I also perform a meditation that is solely focused on space. This meditation can be a little mind-bending, as it challenges your conceptual knowledge of physical space. Visualize yourself growing larger and larger until you become the multiverse itself, filling up every possible star, galaxy, and plane of existence. Now, while keeping that visualization in your mind, also visualize yourself becoming the tiniest particle in existence, shrinking down to the point where you could only be seen on a subatomic level. Then imagine that tiny version of you multiplying, again filling every part of the multiverse, but still being tiny. Now put these two visualizations together. It's pretty mind boggling when you visualize this, but it's similar to the neither-neither principle, where you take two opposite concepts and will them out of existence. You can use the resulting free energy to work some space/time magic. I find in doing this meditation that I become aware of the multiplicity of myself spread throughout the multiverse, as well as the complex nature of the multiverse, because I know even my visualizations are just models that I'm using to represent the multiverse. Even so, those models make me think about what the multiverse has to offer to me.

Another approach to space/time meditation work is Brian Shaughnessy's tesser-act. The tesser-act is a technique in which you visualize yourself in a flower of kairos, a geometric shape that looks like a flower. (To see the actual shape, I suggest readers pick up *Konton* magazine issue 1, which is available through http://www.chaosmagic.com.) The flower of kairos essentially is the container of the tesser-act, where the actual magic occurs. The actual technique involved with the tesser-act varies, depending on what the magician seeks to do:

> Any object inside the tesser-act is bound in that 'otherness,' thus any entity is evoked completely separated from the Magickian, but able to communicate with the Magickian. In this function the tesser-act is a Magickal prison, like the triangle of art. The Magickian may also opt to enter the tesser-act. In this function the tesser-act is a magical liberation, as it allows the Magickian's consciousness to travel through time, and throughout all realms of possibilities.
>
> (Tesseract Magick - 2004, *Brian Shaughnessy*, p. 46)

My experiments mainly involved working with the tesser-act directly, as opposed to using an entity. In working directly with the tesser-act, the ideal goal would be to use it to make yourself aware of possibilities you want to manifest, and then use the tesser-act to materialize those possibilities into the here and now reality. Below is one of the approaches I devised for working with Shaughnessy's technique.

I used the flower of kairos (which is the visualization of the container of the tesser-act) with a ouija board. I painted the design of the flower of kairos from page 46 of *Konton*, issue one, onto my ouija board. (If you attempt this method, use paints that can be wiped off with a damp cloth, in case you would want to use the ouija board for other purposes.) My goal was to take the concept of the ouija as a gateway and enhance it with the flower of kairos. At the same time, by painting the board with the flower of kairos design, I felt I had a very effective visual aide that would help me with the visualization of the flower. Finally, I placed the marker for the ouija board at the center of the flower of kairos. The marker acts as a scrying tool, through which you can either look into the flower, or project yourself into it.

I used this variant technique to do retroactive magic. With my hands on the planchette I projected myself into the flower of kairos. I then visited moments in my past and viewed possibilities that I could use to change my past, to change aspects of myself that I felt needed to be changed. I then merged the past possibility into myself, with the understanding that I had changed myself. I had changed how I'd behaved or acted as a result of incorporating the past into myself. I found that using the tesseract in this manner was highly effective for behavior modification.

Another way to approach space/time is through invocation. My approach to this technique does not incorporate the usual method of invoking an entity into myself. Instead, I invoke myself into the entity or, for that matter, a person. And when invoking into a person, the space/time magic really comes into play. I find that when I perform this technique, I'm not merely accessing that person's mind, but also his/her probability field. To put it another way, I'm aware of all the probable versions of that person: past, present, and future. This occurs because I mesh my energy with their energy, and accordingly I am "reading" their connection to everything around them, which includes space/time. I am present in all moments in which that person or deity exists. No person is ever unconnected from the multiverse, although some connections differ from others. Through the connection that you and I have with the multiverse we can perceive the probabilities for each other.

A fun exercise involves doing this technique of invocation with a partner. Find someone you trust, and then invoke yourself into them. At the same time, the partner should invoke him/herself into you. What I've found happens is that, even though both people are invoking each other, there is still a sense of connection and exploration within each person. After all, magic isn't limited to a specific space or time. And in the case of invoking yourself into someone else, you are still present for that person to invoke him/herself into you. This invocation into the self is very useful for a number of purposes, including helping someone uproot aspects of the psyche. This exercise is useful for space/time magic when it synthesized with a meditative approach. The two paradigms I've mentioned above are useful for this work, but if you have your own approach, certainly use that.

Here's how this technique works when it comes to space/time magic. For the purposes of initial experimentation, tell your partner of a specific probability of reality that you want invoked into yourself. Your partner should also tell you a specific probability that s/he wants invoked. Now invoke yourselves into each other. At this point, you are part of each other's connection to the multiverse. Now visualize the specific paradigm of choice that you use for your space/time meditations, but do so for your partner. (For instance, using the I.T. approach, I'll see a bunch of bubbles that pertain to the life of the individual into whom I'm invoked.) You know the specific probability your partner wants invoked into reality. Focus on finding that probability, and when you do find it, direct it toward them. How you do that is up to you. Sigils are one way of doing so, but another way could be that you visualize the probability going into your partner and manifesting in their life. When you come out of the trance describe what you did for your partner and then both of you should keep watch and find out if the specific probability manifests into your lives.

Another way to use this method of invocation involves invoking yourself into you. That might sound contradictory, but I've always felt that there is a multiplicity of selves, of probable selves, within us. We can access those probable selves through meditation, and this invocation technique is one way of doing that. When I invoke myself into me or, for that matter, into another person I always use the phrase: "I invoke myself into [full name of person]." The phrase is simply my way of focusing my consciousness on the task at hand. You can use it, or another one, or none at all, again depending on your approach to magic. When I invoke myself into me, I focus on contacting one of the multiple versions of myself. That version represents the reality I want to manifest into my life. Accordingly, when I find that version, I merge with that alternate self and bring it into this reality. In essence, I become the alternate version. In doing so, I manifest that probability into reality.

Another way to work with space/time magic is through evocation, again with the idea being to evoke a probability, as opposed to an entity. A definition of classic evocation is the following: "Evocation can be defined as the calling forth of an entity from another plane of existence to an external manifestation in either the astral or physical plane. Evoked beings are brought closer to a magician, but never within him or herself" (Summoning Spirits – 1995, *Konstantinos*, p. 5). In my case, I don't evoke the entity; I evoke the concept or possibility that I want to bring into reality, focusing on manifesting it around me. Even though I'm not calling on an entity, I am still moving through the astral and mental realms to find and then call forth the possibility into material reality. Evocation of this type doesn't involve meditation per se, but I do find meditating on the probability useful as a way of preparing for the evocation. You need, after all, to have a really good visualization of how the possibility will manifest, as well as how you'll deal with it. Usually in my meditations I give the probability a specific form. A sigil could be used, but I'll also use an everyday object as a focus. For instance, a book can represent an evocation of a possibility. Or you can just focus on the effect, the probability manifesting, and let *that* be your evocation. There's something to be said for evoking the effect desired, without necessarily going through a convoluted process of calling an entity to do so.

Whatever you decide to use for your evocation, consider that you will need to do some form of visualization that well help create the desired evocation. Gray's concept of Telesmic Images may be exactly what's called for:

> A so-called Telesmic Image (or TI for short) is a perfectly genuine Inner construction of Force and Form, designed for a particular purpose and having as much, if not more, reality in its own dimensions than we have in Outer terms. It is a composite creation, brought into being as a concretion of consciousness inspired by spirit, animated by soul, moulded by mind, and based upon body. A TI is in fact made up very much as we are ourselves, except that it objectifies on levels of existence that to us are subjective. Its main function is that of an operative focus between our Inner and Outer states of Being.
>
> (Inner Traditions of Magic - 1970, *William G, Gray,* p. 13)

For some people (and this includes myself), the use of evocation involves manifesting the internal externally. By that I mean I manifest the force within me through evocation. Gray's concept of TI is useful in helping us understand the process, as well as how it can be applied to space/time magic probabilities. The fact that TI can be used to objectify a probability is very useful for a magician. Sometimes, you can become too attached to the probabilities you wish to manifest, and that subjectivity consequently creates havoc in the magic working you seek to do. An evocation, using TI, can distance you from the situation, creating enough objectivity for the magic to work and the result to manifest. The TI is your evocation, your composite creation of the probability you wish to manifest into reality. The inner form is manifested outward through the realization of the TI, and this is done by calling the TI (in this case a desired probable reality) into existence.

I evoke my probabilities with several different techniques. One technique is creating artwork or paintings. The earlier chapter on painting discussed how I go about creating the paintings and use them to manifest my probabilities, but I want to touch briefly on the concept of evocation in this act. The painting is a medium, a bridge if you will, between the immaterial world and the material world. It represents the desire both as concept and actualized reality. The painting has its own reality, its own existence, and functions as a TI precisely because it acts as a mediation on reality, superimposing my desired probability into the actual reality, and consequently remaking reality with that probability manifested. The painting externalizes, evokes what I seek to call forth and make reality.

Another way I evoke probabilities is more meditative and very pleasurable. Sex magic, whether it's with a partner or by yourself, tends to be a generator of energy. We all know this. But it's a question of what to do with that energy. Sometimes, to energize a probability into reality, I use sex magic as a way of evoking it. Once the orgasm has been reached, I'll sometimes find myself in a pleasant meditative after state, halfway between sleep and wakefulness. I use that state of mind to evoke the probability I seek to manifest into reality. Sometimes I'll use my cum as the medium for that expression, but other times I'll simply focus on visualizing the reality externally manifesting, and then visualize how I react to that reality. I find that in doing this, I'm effectively evoking the reality and my response to it, and usually when the reality manifests, it does so in accordance with the sex magic visualization that I've done.

I also find with evocation that what is being called into existence has its own consciousness, and this applies to the probabilities that I call forth, as well as any demon, entity, or other being I might conjure up to work with. Any probability, just by being perceived, has come into existence within your life, and that existence has consciousness, has purpose: "Each Image has its particular type of consciousness which it embodies and expresses. We might equally say that every specialized type of consciousness produces its own particular 'Image' or reaction in perceptual terms to those Life-Entities making use of it, including ourselves" (Inner Traditions of Magic - 1970, *William G, Gray,* p. 13). The evocation of that probability also brings that consciousness into your life. The end result is not only the realization of a specific desire, but also the awareness that, as we shape probabilities into reality, they shape the reality of us into probability. After all, the realization of one probability into reality also brings awareness (hopefully) of new opportunities.

Yet another way I use evocation for probabilities involves what I call passive evocation. This is using synchronicities to evoke specific patterns of reality, or as I put it, instead of letting synchronicities happen to you, let you happen to the synchronicities. First of all, you have to observe or be aware of a specific pattern in your life that you want to change or cultivate. For instance, I wanted to meet more magicians in the local area, and perhaps even get into a community. Since it was the beginning of the school semester, I knew I'd meet lots of new people, including, potentially, fellow magicians. And once I met a magician, a pattern of energy, a synchronicity that would bring us together would occur, and I could evoke or replicate that pattern simply by being aware of it, copying the energy and sending it outward to evoke more meetings. And that's exactly what happened in the Fall of 2004. I had several "chance" meetings with people, and I used the energy, the awareness of the pattern leading up to the meeting, and replicated it by using my intuition.

Passive evocation relies upon intuition. You should use it as a tool to follow the patterns that will create what it is you seek. In other words, you are opening yourself up to the patterns of energy that can lead you to what you desire. When my intuition went off, and told me in one way or another to go to a specific place, or say something to a specific person, I did so, and each time I met another magician, and eventually evoked the community I wanted to join, as I was ultimately introduced to one in the local area. I didn't actively evoke the probability by visualizing it. Instead, I just made myself aware of how the possibility of meeting someone manifested into reality, and I duplicated that effect by using my intuition to home in on the energy of the manifestation. Other people who've tried this technique have found that it works rather well for evoking probabilities based on patterns of behavior, or other patterns that exist.

One final evocation technique to bring probabilities into reality is meditation. I've mentioned a variant of it already with sex magic, but the Offnung meditation works just as well. When you're meditating, and using a specific paradigm of your choice or making, you can include this task: When you've picked the probability you've decided to manifest into your life, go into it and live that probability, but while you're doing that, project the living of this probability into the external world. The energy you send into the external world will eventually manifest into reality.

Regardless of which technique of meditation or ritual magic you apply to manifesting your probabilities, the most important aspect of all the procedures is that they work, and that you understand how they work. Knowing how to manifest the probability is the key to manifesting it when you need it, not just when you want it.

Something else that is almost as important is containment or limitation. With the science paradigms from the last chapter and the meditation techniques from this chapter, it becomes very easy to tap into what seem like unlimited probabilities. I have to admit that at times, when I've done the Offnung technique, I've felt overwhelmed by all those probabilities. I've almost felt as if I could drown in the opportunities and choices I could make. And that can be a problem, because it can lead to indecision. Being indecisive, as you know, is being unable to make a choice, embark on an action, etc. This is a danger for the space/time magician, especially at the beginning, when s/he is just beginning to perceive all the past, present, and future probabilities. But how do you avoid feeling overwhelmed?

This is where the benefit of containment or limitation comes into play. Although you can access a seemingly unlimited field of probabilities, for all intents and purposes you don't really need to. If your purpose is to explore a specific incident in your life, or engineer the manifestation of a specific probability, then you'll want to limit what you're doing to those specifics. This can be achieved several ways. First, you can sigilize the probability, and then use that sigil as a guide to find the probability. The sigil acts as both a descriptor and proscriptor of the probability. You know how to find the probability, and you already have a good idea of how it will be limited. The purpose of the meditation, in this case, is just to double-check the probability you're manifesting into reality. It's always good, after all, to have an idea of the effects you can anticipate.

The second way is to visualize a limited field of probabilities. You might not be able to be very specific. Perhaps you don't know all the details about a specific probability, or you want to examine related opportunities that might be more favorable than the specific probability you're thinking of manifesting. In this case, visualizing a set of probabilities, all related to each other, can be useful. I sometimes even find myself visualizing different outtakes on the same probability, which is useful not only for acquiring an awareness of potential consequences, but also as a good perception exercise.

A third method involves giving the probability a material form. This is one reason why I paint a lot of the space/time magic I do. The process of painting allows me to interact with the creative, intuitive realms of consciousness, but at the same time it also allows me to limit that realm to the painting itself. Writing can also act as a similar medium. Really, any form of expression can be used to limit what you work with. Limitation, in its own way, gives a person power:

> Imagine trying to make Jell-o without a container or perhaps trying to carry a gallon of water without something to carry it in...If you tried to gather a gallon of water from a lake with no means to separate that gallon from the rest of the lake, you would understand the power of limitation. Without a container or the power of limitation, we not only would end up with Jell-o all over the place, but also with a non-expression of Jell-o.
>
> (Meditations on the Cube of Space - 2003,
> *Kevin Townley,* p. 16)

In other words, limitation gives you the power to define what you want to achieve, as well as how to do so. If you look at all of the techniques in this book you'll quickly realize that there is limitation involved, but that it serves a purpose. That purpose is to help you avoid indecision, to find opportunity, and otherwise benefit from using the techniques.

You probably know people in your life who've been raised without much limitation from their parents. These people tend to be indecisive, doing little with their lives, in large part because they've never had limitations imposed upon them. Now granted this isn't true for all people who've been raised without limitations, but my point is that limitation is ultimately an empowering principle of life. It serves to direct and focus us on overcoming the obstacles. I know that any time I've been limited I've wanted to challenge those limits or learn to use them for my benefit. You can apply this principle of limitation and its use to space/time magic. As I mentioned above, it's very easy to be overwhelmed by the endless possibilities, but by applying limitation, whether it's through technique or the realization that you only need to deal with specific probabilities, you can get more out of space/time magic than by dealing with unlimited expanses of probabilities. Still, sometimes it can be fun to drift in such an endless sea of probabilities. Just know when to limit yourself, so you're not too caught up in it.

Exercises

1. Either use of the paradigms for meditation I mention above or come up with one of your own that you can use to work space/time magic. How effective are the paradigms for you? How would you modify my paradigms, or, for that matter, your own?

2. Try out the invocation or evocation techniques. With the invocation exercise, try it out with a friend and make sure you both note results. Again, how would you modify these techniques?

3. Try to think of ways limitation has benefited you in your life, as well as how it could be applied to space/time workings in a manner I might not have considered.

Chapter Ten:
Magic and Technology

The preceding chapter focused on meditation. You might wonder, then, why I've made technology the final chapter of the book. I've found, sometimes for myself, and sometimes for other people, that technology can be useful for enhancing meditations. It can also be a useful medium for explaining and exploring principles of space/time magic. As an example, not everyone will easily grasp nonlinear thinking, as some people are so conditioned to linear thinking that they don't readily grasp or understand the alternative. I know it took me years to understand and integrate a non-linear way of thinking, and to thereby understand perceived reality. Accordingly, some aspects of this chapter are an attempt to help some readers understand the concepts through concrete examples, while other aspects are focused on extending the techniques from the last chapter, by using technology.

One of the most fascinating aspects of the computer is its ability to multitask. We can open a fair number of programs and utilize them at the same time. The downside is that the more programs you open up, the longer it takes the computer to finish its various tasks. Nonetheless, this paradigm of multitasking is useful for us to adopt. Humans, in general, are capable of multitasking, but not with the apparent ease of a computer. Still, if we use the computer as a mindset, we can create for ourselves a multitasking "program" that allows us to surf the probabilities of space/time, as well as attending to other matters. I liken this kind of program to having a bunch of avatars or programs that handle each task, all at the same time. I visualize different versions of myself that use my brain as a computer in order to work on different tasks at the same time. If you think about it, we do this constantly with our body in any case. How many people take the time to think about the fact that they are breathing or that their hearts are beating? The answer is we don't. Our heartbeats or our breathing are programs we run automatically, albeit we can take over and consciously control how deeply we breathe or how fast our hearts beat. Nonetheless, most people don't spend a lot of time focusing on these programs or others.

How does this relate to space/time magic? Being able to multi-task is being able to think and work in a non-linear manner. Using the computer as a paradigm, or for that matter the television, can be a useful way of understanding non-linear thinking. We know that every channel, show or commercial on a television is being broadcast at the same time. Using a remote control allows us to flip back and forth, but the program will continue to show even when we're not watching it. The other interesting aspect about the television is that it can show us different versions of reality, to which Genesis P-orridge can aptly attest from when he first met William S. Burroughs: "'Well...Reality is not all it's cracked up to be you know,' he continued. He took the remote and started to flip through the channels, cutting up programmed TV...At the same time he began to hit stop and start on his Sony TC cassette recorder, mixing in 'random' cut-up prior recordings. These were overlaid with our conversation, none acknowledging the other, an instant holography of information and environment" (Book of Lies: The Disinformation Guide to Magick and the Occult - 2003, *Genesis P-orridge,* p. 105-106). As Genesis found, the television and other forms of media could not only be used to rewrite reality, but also in and of themselves represented different versions of reality, all happening at the same time. Likewise with a computer, we aren't aware of all the programs running at the same time. Nonetheless, there are programs running that the computer uses to complete tasks that allow us to use other programs. If we apply this understanding to ourselves, we can appreciate how to utilize multi-tasking in our lives.

Multi-tasking is possible for people. Consider that, while you might have to direct your conscious attention toward a specific goal at a given time, it is still possible to direct your sub-consciousness toward multiple other goals. You simply have to make yourself aware of those goals first. For instance, one reason I write notes on little sticky paper pads is to remind myself of things I need to do or finish. Some part of me is processing the information for the task so that when I need to do the task I'm ready to do it quickly and efficiently. Those sticky notes serve as reminders to the subconscious to fully activate that program.

Beyond looking at a computer as a paradigm for non-linear thought, one specific program people may find useful for doing space/time work is Winamp, particularly using it as a way of translating sound into color and shape. The colors and shapes can be used as gateways or means of going into trance by triggering altered states of mind. Winamp translates the music you listen to into color and shape. I do use other tools than Winamp for this purpose, but Winamp has one benefit that the other tools do not: it creates specific shapes, so that, for instance, you can create a vortex image and use it to put yourself into a trance. After doing that, you simply allow yourself, in your altered state of consciousness, to experience space/time as multiple possibilities, intuitively seeking out the best possibilities for yourself. Also with the shapes you create, you can make specific gateways to specific probabilities or other planes of existence. This is similar to the use of Tattvas, which are cards with specific colors and shapes that can be used by the magician to visualize a gateway to an elemental realm or some other conceptual realm of magic. In any case, Winamp is an effective tool for meditation/trance work, and it's free to download, which is another benefit for the magician who has a computer, but who might not have funds for other technological gadgets that can be used for these kinds of workings.

I mentioned the television above in regards to the paradigm, but it also has other uses for space/time magic. For instance, I find the remote controller of the television extremely handy as a magical wand. With the push of a button an appliance is turned on or off. With other buttons we can adjust the volume, or flip randomly through channels, creating our own virtual reality or realities, as the case may be. When the television is connected to other appliances it can add other facets of "reality" to the mix: DVDs, where the past can be revisited with the touch of a button, or video games where virtual environments enthrall players. I find that flipping randomly through TV channels is not merely an effective way of doing divination, but can also help with understanding non-linear reality, as mentioned above. Channel-flipping can also be of benefit when you're charging a sigil. Flip to a channel, watch it for a bit, while the fascination lasts, and draw the energy of that fascination into a sigil. Then flip to the next channel and start a new sigil. Channel switching can be an effective way to use your attention as a way of charging and firing sigils. As you watch the TV, superimpose the image of the sigil onto the screen, until the only reality you see is the sigil and the probability it represents. Flip to a new channel and repeat. Again, direct the attention you give to the show to forming the sigil that gradually feeds off the energy of the show to manifest the probability you're working with.

This sigil technique works in a similar way to the comic's panel technique mentioned earlier, but the difference is that you use the channels and the television screen as your panel. The remote controller can be useful as a tool for envisioning the charging of the sigil. For instance, you can trace the sigil on the screen mentally, but use the controller as the tracer. Given that the controller emits energy to change a channel, the principle of using the controller to trace the sigil is that you're accessing the concept of it, and creating the sigil through the energy it emits. When you change the channel, you've moved from one panel to the next. You can always go back, though.

With this kind of sigil work you harness the energy of the television shows, stations, even cable or satellite to charge and fire the sigil. Also, you broadcast your magic through these media, so it's not simply you who charges and fires, but also the masses who choose to watch a program at the same time you do. They don't see the sigil, nor are they even aware of it, but they give their attention to the show or shows that you're using to charge and fire your sigils. And that attention adds up to a lot of energy going into your sigil.

Although I've covered how to use video games as a form of magic in pop culture, something I've noticed lately that pertains more to space/time magic is the number of games based on historic periods of the past, and games that are similar to the "choose your own adventure" booklets. To play these, you choose a "path," but then have to make another choice so that another path opens up. A video game such as *Way of the Samurai 2* can be instructive to the nature of space/time, shattering the illusion of linear reality, by showing a person how the choices s/he makes can open up opportunities, even as some of those choices can negate opportunity for them. And while a video game is just a game, the concept to be derived from it is that space/time is flexible in reality as well, provided you're aware of the choices you're making, and the consequences for those choices. The lesson here is that opportunities are made by the choices we make, the perceptions we cultivate. A lot of the video games available now tend to lean toward a more non-linear approach to gaming. You can always go back and play that last level again before you progress, but even within the game you'll have options where, if you succeed in a mission, another one will open up, or if you fail in a mission, yet another one will open up. *Samurai Warriors* is a good example of that kind of video game. And while retroactive magic might not be that easy, you always have the opportunity to re-examine how you acted in a situation, and change yourself as a result of that.

The point I'm really making about technology is that it provides its own tricks and understanding of the flexibility of time. We just have to be receptive to that understanding. Everything is recorded, so cut it up and rearrange the recordings, rearrange space/time, and manifest your own reality. Video games can be one way of doing that, and we owe it to ourselves to explore the potential they offer us. Another way to look at it is that games like these can teach us a lot about opportunity, and the importance of awareness in finding it. The more aware you are of how to trigger an event, the easier it is to do so, and that's true in both a game and everyday life.

I've dealt with some miscellaneous approaches to technology and space/time. But as I mentioned above there are tools you can use to aid you in meditation. Winamp is one. The dream machine and audiostrobe mind machines are another. Both of these technologies use the flicker principle:

> Flicker is the application of pulsed light to the optical region with eyes either open or closed. Research has shown that in most people flicker produces extraordinary responses in the brain. This is because the light signal causes a coded message to be distributed to its every part...The peculiar feature of flicker stimulation is that anyone looking at the light soon begins to see more than just a flicker. There is a sensation of movement, pattern, and changing color. The unexpected bonus is that the fantastic designs, movements of color and sensations of bodily involvements are in the mind of the perceiver, this also supplies a clue as to his creative potential.
>
> (TAGC-Teste Tone Liner Notes)

Flicker allows you to access different layers of consciousness, uniting the sub-conscious with the conscious through the manipulation of light and sound. I've used both a dream machine and a mind machine, and have found that the music I listen to can affect the patterns I perceive in the light. Volume can also have an effect. Anyone who has epilepsy should not use either machine, as they can induce epileptic seizures. Fortunately, for the rest of us these machines can be used to good effect.

There are advantages and disadvantages to each machine. You can find plans for the dream machine on the Internet. Simply type in "dream machine" on a search engine. To make the dream machine requires a decent knowledge of math, a 78 rpm record player (not easy to find these days), several sheets of black cardboard or foam board (one that you can make mistakes on and trace/cut out for the other board), and a record you never want to play again. It also requires the time to make it. The advantage of the dream machine is that it's cheap to make, and if you make it properly you can avoid a side effect I'll mention in a moment.

It's also a great conversation starter, and can be fun to use at parties or with a couple friends that come over (but this also true of the mind machine). The disadvantage is that it's not necessarily easy to lug the dream machine around. You have to be careful when moving any of the equipment for it, if only because if you drop something – such as the record player – you need to buy another one. But given the overall cheapness of making the dream machine, this isn't a big deal...unless you can't find any record players. If the dream machine isn't constructed properly, you can suffer the occasional bout of depression after using it, but this only occurs if you botch the making of the cylinder. If this happens, make another cylinder and be careful with the measurements. The first time I used a dream machine I did get depressed, but subsequent uses with a correctly made machine gave me no problems.

The mind machine is essentially similar to the dream machine. It has several advantages, however. It's small and easy to carry around. It comes with a set of headphones and a pair of LED audiostrobe glasses. Depending on the version you acquire, you can get a lot of useful features. Also, I've yet to get depressed after using a mind machine. However, as with all things, there is a disadvantage as well. The cost is a bit high. You end up forking out over a hundred dollars, and possibly up to two hundred dollars. Also, depending on the version you get, you could be paying more and getting fewer features. As an example, the Proteus model is the most expensive version. However, an informed buyer would choose the cheaper Sirius model, and here's why.

The Proteus allows you to download new programs and change them around; basically, you can tinker with them. However, it doesn't have features that the Sirius has, which in my opinion makes the Sirius a better buy. With the Sirius you don't have to just play audio-technology CDs. These are CDs made specifically for use with a mind machine that trigger the machine to start flickering when you play them. You might not want to buy these special purpose CDs. You might have music, as I do, that you feel will produce a similar effect. With the Sirius you can actually play other CDs, and the audiostrobe glasses will take the sounds and turn them into light impulses. Also, the Sirius has a built in microphone, so you can take it to a concert and use it there. In my opinion, the Sirius is best mind machine to buy. I own both a mind machine and a dream machine, and I switch between them, using one or the other.

The benefit of using this technology, beyond having a trip without a drug, is that it can stimulate creativity and learning. I know that when I have writer's block, taking a break on the dream or mind machine clears the block, and the writing flows. These machines tap into the subconscious, allowing you to access your creative and intuitive aspects, as well as allowing access to space/time probabilities. For the Sirius mind machine, I recommend program seventeen for getting rid of writer's block.

As I've mentioned before in this book, I think that by accessing different states of consciousness we alter our perception of space/time, and get glimpses of probabilities; we exist in a different state from the conceptual "normal" state we live in. It's intriguing to note that Nostradamus experienced his visions on top of a tower, where he would place his hands over his face and move his fingers rapidly in front of his eyes, producing patterns which he used to read the future. Given that a fair amount of his predictions have apparently come true, the flicker effect can be used as a method of scrying. But you can extend the use of the mind machine past scrying. In general I find that I don't use these machines for divinations, so much as for shaping probabilities.

When looking into the dream machine or LED glasses the eyes should be closed. You'll see light, and after a short time patterns and images will appear. When using the machines, I find that certain music will produce certain specific images. For instance, listening to The Swans always connects me to symbols of Gnostic Christianity. You may or may not note similar effects. In any case, when you look into either machine, patterns will begin to form. You can use these patterns to understand the nature of probabilities. Focus on a pattern and then try to change it while using the technology. Inevitably, I find that the patterns change and continue to change, even after I stop directing those changes. Perhaps it's my subconscious coming through. What I also find with these patterns is that they do have meaning. For instance, when using the mind machine I've seen a spiral strand within which are bubbles of probabilities. I'll actually see those possibilities play out between the flickers of light, seeing glimpses of what might be. As you continue to work with the machines, you can learn to direct your attention to those probabilities, so that you can actually explore them with your mind. Altering the frequencies of the light pulses helps with this kind of work, but it's also beneficial to learn to use the patterns that the light creates, to keep you focused on the possibility you're exploring, as you incorporate the light patterns into creating the reality you want to manifest. In the end, this technique is simply about taking a distraction, such as the flickering of the lights, and learning to use it to aid you in the manifestation of a probability into reality. For all intents and purposes, my paradigms have been visually created by my interaction with the machine. Also, because your subconscious is accessed through the flicker effect, you can get some intense visualizations of past, present, and future events. I've sometimes found that using the machines is a good way of triggering a specific memory, and so sometimes I'll use them for retroactive magic. I visualize that I project myself into the memories I recall and then change those memories by changing the patterns of light. I then impress those changed patterns into the memory, via the meditation I'm performing.

I think the best aspect about using these machines is that they can help you, particularly if you're first starting out with meditations and are not having much success. Using one of the machines will allow you to visualize the space/time probabilities you're working with a bit more easily, so that you can get a visual sense of your paradigm. This can be invaluable, especially for people who are very linear in their thinking, and who might not have much experience with meditation. I find that, when I use the machines, I can easily mold and work with the patterns that I see, and the results of using the machines have always been favorable.

However, it's also important not to rely too heavily on a tool. Learning to improve your natural meditative ability is something you should cultivate as much as possible. I can say that my natural meditations tend to be more intense and last longer than the meditations I use with either machine. This is partially due to the non-linear thinking I've embraced. With the mind machine, in particular, but also with the dream machine, there tends to be a time limit, usually when the sound stops. With my natural meditations I've found they tend to last longer. I also go into a deeper trance. Remember that no tool is a substitute for practice. It's taken me years of dedication with the Offnung technique to experience the kind of meditations I have now, but that investment of effort has clearly been worth it. By developing your own abilities, and not relying too heavily on tools such as machines or drugs, you will be able to truly understand the depth of your consciousness and how you can access space/time through the alteration of consciousness.

You might note I haven't mentioned the use of drugs in space/time magic. I don't use drugs; in fact the few experiences I've had with them have ultimately been rather negative. Perhaps this was due to the tinkering I'd already done with my electro-chemistry, or perhaps it was just the experiences themselves. Accordingly, I haven't experimented with drugs to do space/time workings. I am sure others have, and if you wish to, you can. That is your personal choice, though do be aware of the legal ramifications of what you do. I can say, for myself, that I am comfortable using the mind machines and my meditation techniques for the space/time work I've been doing.

In the appendix on pop culture and magic, I'll present a ritual in which you can use one of the machines for your ritual. At this point, remember that, ideally, magic progresses with the times. Learning to use and understand technology in your magical workings is essential for the evolution of magicians. It's also handy to be more technologically savvy than other people, as it can put you in a position of leadership in the world outside the magical community. These kinds of positions are important for the growth of the magical community. But again, what is more important is that your magical practices evolve, and using technology is part of that evolution.

Exercises

1. Try to do the sigil technique I mention in this chapter, in regards to television channels and remote controls. Is this sigil technique as effective as other techniques mentioned in the chapter on space/time sigils? Why or why not?

2. If possible, either make a dream machine or acquire a mind machine. Then experiment with the machine, with the purpose being to experience a meditative state similar to the ones described in chapter nine. Then meditate without the machine, again with the focus being to attain a meditative state described in chapter nine. In your opinion, which method is better, and why?

3. I mentioned the possibility of using the machines to do retroactive magic. How would you apply the machines to a retroactive ritual?

4. How might you combine using these machines with other techniques mentioned in previous chapters...for example, painting or artwork?

5. Do you or the mind machine produce the patterns that you see in it? Support your answer with whatever evidence you can amass from your experiments.

Epilogue

In reading this book, I hope you've acquired some useful techniques and insights that you can apply to space/time magic. My goal with this book is the same as with *Pop Culture Magick*. I want to promote creativity and open-mindedness in my fellow magicians. Take these techniques and improve on them. I look forward to hearing how you've changed them, improved them, and otherwise achieved the goals you've wanted to achieve. While it's important to acknowledge our roots, to acknowledge the shoulders we've stood upon (just look at the bibliography for this book to see that principle in action!), it's also important to progress, to evolve our practices. We cannot afford to be dogmatic and stagnant, close-minded and foolish, because of how outlandish someone's ideas appear to be.

My encounters with dogmatic magicians have inevitably shown me that they often mistake the example for the technique, and if someone writes a book on a subject that is deemed outlandish, despite how "open-minded" they claim to be, they'll inevitably resort to ridicule, without necessarily reading what's there. This trend needs to stop. You don't have to agree with the examples that a magician uses, but explore the technique behind the example and improve upon it. Likewise, if an idea seems outlandish, it may very well be that, but check it out anyway. You never know what you can learn from even the most outlandish ideas and approaches to magic or, for that matter, life. If we don't attempt to understand, we create ignorance in our lives, and that ignorance leads to stagnancy. For me, at least, magic is not about stagnancy, but about challenging the self and growing as an individual, and, potentially, as a community. It's also about challenging the traditions you come from, testing the limits, and doing something new. And who cares if, in the end, it's a reinvention of the wheel. Better to do that than to stick with what other people have done. Doing magic a bit differently is a thrill for its own sake. We lose this thrill when we dourly glance at someone experimenting and say that person shouldn't do this or that, or say s/he's reinventing the wheel, or that someone is deluded because s/he chooses not to utilize a traditional method of magic. This cynical and unfounded attitude needs to go away. It has no place in the heart, mind, and soul of the true magician.

This book is the result of a lot of experimentation and work over the years. I've always found the concept of space/time magic intriguing. But something I've realized is that, while the techniques are important, what is even more important is the relationship you develop with the multiverse. Working on the ideas in this book has been a truly spiritual experience and evolution for me. Occasionally it's been comfortable, but more often than not it's been challenging. But I wouldn't have it any other way. It's through challenges that we grow, and there truly is nothing more exhilarating than doing that. I know I've bonded with the multiverse, found myself coming closer to a feeling of belonging. The words I've written, the techniques I've developed, cannot express the ineffable experiences I've had. They can, at best, describe concepts, but the actual experience is something so intangible it almost seems it's not real, until you realize with a start that it is real, precisely because you are shaping your reality with what you do and experience. I hope this work does the same for you.

The appendices that follow this epilogue are some miscellaneous ideas related to space/time magic. I suppose some of them could have been chapters in their own right, but I feel they work well as appendices, and I imagine you'll find them useful for supplementing what you've read in this book. May the work you do with this book be creative and innovative and for the good of magic.

My next book will be on DNA magic and inner alchemy. Until then, may your travels in space/time be as fruitful and fun as my own.

Appendix A
A Space/Time Death-Rebirth Ritual

One of the great themes of magical life is death-rebirth. I have now experienced six death-rebirths. Some of those experiences have not been overtly magical (such as a car accident I was in), but nonetheless served as catalytic events. Some experiences, such as the one I will now discuss, have been overtly magical. All of them have affected my life.

This ritual of space/time death-rebirth began February 1st 2004, and lasted for two days. It utilized several principles, which worked for me. I do not suggest that what worked for me will work for everyone, as my methods were, in some ways, highly personal.

Before February 1st, I had been dealing with the concept of community and my own attempts to grapple with what that is. My posts on community as well as a dialogue on the ritual as it was happening over the course of two days can be found at http://www.livejournal.com/users/teriel/. Those interested in reading the logs should start from February 1st through February 4th of 2004. The purpose of my death-rebirth ritual was not just to end my life and have a rebirth, but also to purge the feelings of alienation and anger I'd felt over having no community. Surprisingly enough, other people responded, and in a sense this ritual became their ritual as much as mine.

This space/time ritual can be used for anything and can be adapted in anyway, shape or form. What matters most is that you stay true to the concepts being explored.

The Path of Poison and Inner Alchemy

On February 1st, around eleven at night, I put *Psychic TV- the Black Concert* in my VCR and began watching it, while I painted a sigil that represented all the feelings I felt. I listened to this concert three times, using the energy of it as an effective way of trancing while I painted the sigil. In the midst of that I also began to do some inner alchemy.

Inner alchemy is the ability to manipulate your physiology with a thought. People who have read John Lilly's *Programming the Human Biocomputer* know of his detailed mapping of the brain, and how the brain can be programmed. I recommend this book to any occultist who is interested in inner alchemy. I used this book back in 1997 as a means of learning how to program my own brain, but this quickly led into interests in not only programming the brain, but programming the body. I figured that if we could take drugs to stimulate effects within us, we could likely duplicate those effects without drugs. Meditation is obviously one of way doing this, but inner alchemy, which manipulates the electro-chemistry of the brain, as well as hormonal levels and other physiological aspects, is another way. Drugs essentially stimulate certain portions of the brain to secrete the necessary natural chemical to provide the altered experience. But with inner alchemy is it possible to will yourself to be high or to trip. You simply stimulate the endorphins with a thought. Obviously, inner alchemy has other uses, which I'll get to in a moment.

When I first began programming my brain and body, I did so by narrowing my consciousness down to that of a blood cell in my body. I traveled throughout my body, through all the organs, mapping the energy as well as the way the organs worked. Thus I learned how to stimulate the necessary parts of my body to do what I needed with a thought alone. A useful exercise in controlling your heart can be found in Hereward Carrington and Sylvan Muldoon's *The Art of Astral Projection*. I recommend that exercise as a way to start learning how to do inner alchemy.

Inner alchemy has another benefit, which I used for my death-rebirth ritual. Once you have experienced a state of being, you can call it forth at any time. I called forth a drug overdose that I'd experienced at the previous death-rebirth ritual that I went through. In that particular case, I'd been given an herbal potion by a Native American shaman. He and I drank the potion, did a sex magic ritual, and when it culminated, the potion kicked in. My experience at that time was of my body falling part, swirling away into nothingness. For this ritual of February 1st I invoked that same experience, descending into the path of poison.

A mentor of mine in State College, Pennsylvania, introduced the path of poison as a form of magic to me in 1998. It is destruction for the magician, but revelatory destruction. We poison ourselves in an effort to find destruction, but within that destruction also lies purging and purification. I am not nearly as dedicated as my friend was to the path of poison. For me, it is an occasional path to descend and earn the purging I need through my own destruction. For him it was much more. I wish to state that I do not advocate this form of magic as being for just anyone. It requires discipline and experience, and is not an easy path to tread. Although I've only used this path occasionally, I have never done it casually. I've been able work with this path of magic because I've worked a lot with the physiology of my body, and worked with it, in this case, to induce a near death experience. I take no responsibility for anyone who should choose to try the path on the basis of my writings, as it is YOUR choice to do so.

I invoked the path of poison, and in particular, the withdrawal experience I went through after the drug wore off (from the previous near death experience with the shaman). My body started to cramp, and I found myself frequently going to the restroom. My feces turned black. I did not feel an urge to throw-up, but the cramps were painful enough, so painful that at times I could not move. When I went to sleep later that night, after completing the painting, I went with the understanding that I was going to a death. Before I actually went to sleep I invoked Euronynmous, a Demonolatry god of the dead. I tranced out and was visited by him with the purpose of taking me to death. I was put in a crypt and left there by him to die. Throughout the night and well into February 2nd I continued to feel cramps as my body continued to poison itself. While all this was occurring, I was also absorbing my energy, the essence of Taylor into myself to gestate, creating room for Zero.

Two aspects of this ritual can be useful. The first is that of inducing a near state of death, but make sure it's a controlled inducement. The second is that a god form of death, or whatever represents death, can be a useful aide in the actual experience of death.

The Invocation of Zero

The near death experience brought on the state of Zero, the state of facelessness. From the 2nd to the 3rd of February I was Zero...both dead and alive, my body a rotting sack of flesh, my emotions removed, for all intents and purposes a faceless entity. The concept of Zero as a form of magic came to me through the writings of William Gray, who, it's fair to say, was one of the forefathers of chaos magic. The best way to understand Zero is through the following explanation:

> Whether it is called 'detachment,' or 'uninvolvement,' or any other term this truly magical art amounts to a control of consciousness on a very high level. We live one level higher than our activities all the time, because we work *on* something *from* somewhere. To fully control happenings on any particular level of existence we must operate on it from another. If we want to become anything, we must also 'not-become' everything else. Before any vessel may be filled with any specific content, it must be empty. Before a single number is countable, Zero must be assumed. No Creation is possible without the Void. [Italics are the author's]
>
> (Magical Ritual Methods – 1969, *William G. Gray*, p. 24)

As Gray says, Zero is detachment. For me, the state of Zero also represents all possibilities and none, as well as being faceless. You cannot have an identity when you are Zero because in being

Zero you are both nothing and everything. Those who can achieve this state have a powerful tool on their sides. I have worked with this concept for many years and have always found it highly effective.

In this case the state of Zero was brought on by the death of my identity. Death serves as a portal to Zero. There are other ways to achieve a state of Zero, but for the purposes of this ritual death allows a quick access to that state. In Zero all possibilities are revealed, but here comes the interesting part. While all things are revealed, once you have a chosen a probability to manifest, you are no longer Zero. You have moved from everything and nothing to something. One other thing about Zeroing: It's very tempting to stay as Zero. During this ritual a strong temptation to avoid feeling came over me. Stay Zero...be all and nothing. Do not let this temptation take you over. Zero is ultimately stasis and its edges are exceedingly sharp.

Rebirth

The final part of the ritual is rebirth. I manifested my rebirth through the invocation of several god forms, in addition to using some other tools. I used the god form of Kiraziel, the Dehar. This particular entity is part of Storm Constantine's Dehara system of magic, and in fact is a being created by me. For those interested in the Dehara system, pick up *Grimoire Dehara: Kaimana*, published by Immanion Press. I also invoked Khepher-Khephri, a god form I'd worked with before, but had not done so for several years. He'd recently manifested in my life before this ritual through the last scarab ring that I found at a metaphysical shop.

Both of these god forms acted as tools, Kiraziel being the guardian of my essence, and Khepher being instrument of rebirth for that essence within my body. Other tools I used were body paints and the *Zos/Kia Live* concert by Coil. The body paints were used to paint sigils of the god forms and lines of energy on my body. The music was chosen for its very primal noise, which I felt best represented the process of birth. I turned off all the lights and lay in the darkness, in the Hanged Man position found on tarot cards.

The first half of the meditation involved Zero being devoured by the best representative of my personal demons. This act of devouring is similar to Tibetan rituals, in which the practitioner is devoured by demons, again all for the purpose of creating a new self. I think that those who engage in this ritual will find that the demons are very personal and ultimately useful in facing your fears, insecurities and so on. Once the Zero was devoured and the demons were banished, the time for rebirth began.

Appropriately enough, this began when the screaming on the *Zos/Kia* album started. The music made the rebirth more realistic, more primal, and consequently more powerful. The actual rebirth is a return of your essence, your energy, with something extra as a result of the ritual. You should feel the energy so much that it seems it could burn the skin off you. This will continue for a while.

Final Thoughts

For me, this was a ritual that worked through space/time. At one point, I noted in my Live Journal that as Zero I am infinite, eternal, and always existing. Beyond that, though, this ritual was done to kick start some probabilities into reality for myself, and for other people. Those probabilities were manifested by a need, in this case a need to find a community. My personal needs were also met in doing this ritual, though not entirely in the manner I expected.

What was most interesting to note were the results that occurred during the ritual. Maryam, one of my significant others, found a community that represented her cultural and magical interests during the two day period of the ritual. She and my other significant other (at the time) had dreams that involved some aspect of the ritual during the two-day period. A student of mine gave me a box of books, and posted on his Live Journal about his own feelings of loneliness, of no community, thus establishing a resonance. Finally on the morning of the final day of the ritual, the bathroom light refused to turn off. Certainly, the interest shown by other people in what I was discussing and working through also stands out as results.

Ultimately, though, this is a long-term ritual, which has continued to have effects down the line. To give you an idea of that, a month after the ritual I became very ill, right after I dropped a very stressful class I was taking at the time. The illness was a result of the stress from that class, and was a much needed purging, but this theme of death, as I came to see it, continued. Soon after the illness, three events occurred in April of that year. Each of these events caused considerable havoc in my life when they first happened. I was dumped by someone I was seeing at the time, I was accused of doing something I did not do, and at the university I was attending, events culminated to a point where I seriously considered leaving the program. Fortunately, in every case, the situation was ultimately resolved in my favor. Over time, I came to understand why the breakup occurred, and focused on aspects of myself that need to be changed for healthier relationships. The second case resolved itself, when my innocence was proven by myself and other people, who vouched for my character. And with the school, I ended up choosing to stay in the program, on the understanding that my work there would focus more on my own interests, namely my writing career, as opposed to the more conventional interests of the program. Also, in the summer of 2004 I resolved all the issues with the various people involved in all the scenarios. But I consider all that happened to be a further manifestation of the death end of the ritual. Clearly, there were elements in my life that were unhealthy for me. To have a true rebirth, those elements either needed to be removed or changed so that they were no longer a burden upon me. And so those parts of my life "died," in order that I could move onto a healthier lifestyle, as well as finding the new perspectives I needed for myself and those situations in my life.

The rebirth portion of the ritual really only began for me in the summer of 2004. During that summer I tried to find a job, and several times did, but ultimately ended up walking out on the jobs. I quickly realized that although on the surface I said I wanted a job, I really didn't. What I really wanted was to write, and in fact the first draft of this book was written that summer. That writing was part of my rebirth, but around that time I also began to do workings with the triple goddess, or rather, the triple goddess chose to manifest in my life at that time. Consequentially, since that first manifestation began I've felt that I'd truly begun the rebirth process of the ritual. This goes to show that a ritual cannot be encased in linear time.

That's why it's a space/time ritual. We invoke ourselves to Zero where all possibilities in all realities stand before us, and we manifest those possibilities by making choices and then living with them through the rebirth. And that process can take months or even years. Do I recommend this ritual to others? Most certainly. Change and adapt as needed. I do once again, however, say that those who choose to do this ritual should understand they take full responsibility for the outcome. It is not my responsibility. May you manifest the reality you need.

Appendix B
Space/Time Magic:

The Importance of Magic Manifesting in its Own Time

While this book deals mostly with techniques for and approaches to space/time magic, I thought I would offer a philosophic perspective on doing rituals in their own time. This is important, because in the current mainstream (and magical) society we live in often emphasizes results over process. We live in a "buy it now" society. Depending on the part of the world you live in, you can order most anything online and get it delivered to you in days. Even when going out for dinner, people have the expectation that food will be on the table instantaneously.

Some would blame this consumer culture on technology, but technology is not to blame. Rather, the blame lies with how people have chosen to use technology, and consequently have taken it for granted. Sadly, most people do not even have a remote grasp of how the technology they use works. Needless to say, understanding how technology works can potentially be a path of personal empowerment, though no guarantee can be given that this empowerment will help you in other ways.

The real root of the problem is that people have no appreciation of time, and this I think is a result of linear time. When people think of time as being sequential, they quickly realize that it is limited, and that it becomes more limited with every moment. Thus the push, particularly in American society, to have everything done as quickly as possible. Chug that food down, do this task as quickly as possible, etc. Ironically, this has only made people more miserable. We feel trapped in the rat races of jobs that eat up more and more of our time, demanding that we sacrifice all we enjoy, just to make enough money to survive, and do little else.

You can see this reflected in people's daily planners, planners so crammed with meetings that even getting together with a friend requires freeing up some time, and jotting the friend's name down in that planner. Look to your wrist and you'll see a manacle of linear time, the watch, ticking ominously away. Every tick is a moment of your life, gone, wasted away. Tick, tick, tick. The movement of the second hand is hypnotic, obsessing us with a fear of death as well as the seemingly inevitable ravages of time. Tick, tick, tick. Throw off your manacle, the watch. Do you really need it?

But I'll be late for my job. Well that's why you keep a clock in your home, to remind you of where you need to be and when, but do you need to carry this reminder on you all the time? Throw off your manacles of linear time and embrace non-linear reality. Stop worrying about when you can free up time and just live your life. Honestly, it's healthier in the short and long run.

And how does all this apply to magic? In magic, particularly results magic, there is a tendency to expect that the result will occur *now*. This tendency is dangerous, showing as it does that you've fallen into the brainwashing of linear time. No result can be measured as occurring at a specific moment of time, and to try to limit magic in such a manner is ultimately to emasculate your workings. Everything, and this includes magic, happens in its own time. The result you expect today might not manifest until tomorrow, or the next day, or next week. But when it results, it will occur precisely because that's when it needs to happen. I can't tell you how many times I've done magic and found that the result occurred much later than I thought it would. But when the result happened, it happened at the right time.

In other words, throw off your expectation, your lust for result. That lust derives from linear time infecting your judgment. Nothing ever needs to happen now, this instant, despite the fact that you or I might wish otherwise. A good example is my Death-Rebirth ritual. The results of that ritual are still coming in, at the time of this writing. We cannot quantify results, though the scientists and academics might challenge us to do so. When you quantify the magic you work, you take the power out of it, turning it into a soulless beast. Why even bother doing the spell, if that's all you're looking for?

When I do rituals, there is no specific time frame for either doing the ritual, or for the manifestation of the results. Some rituals, for me, take months of work and effort, before the effects begin to culminate, as the expression of the ritual meets its maturation in its own time. So take a long hand to your rituals, and stretch them out. Are you really in such a hurry that you can reduce your spirituality to one night? If you are, join the high holiday crowd (the ones who only do "magic" on holidays), and leave magic to the real magicians! That isn't to say all rituals should be long, drawn out affairs. Each ritual has its own time, but learning to think in non-linear terms will tap you into the understanding of the appropriate "length" of time. Truthfully though, there is no length of time for a ritual. The magic we work exists outside space/time. The results that come in are just confirmation that you're doing something right, but the magic is always there, always being worked.

Appendix C
Space/Time Entity Work

My co-written book, *Creating Magickal Entities,* explores in detail the creation of entities, and how they can be used for magic. This appendix won't focus too much on the basics of entity work, accordingly. However space/time entity work is something that has always fascinated me, and I think a look at it is worthwhile.

One of the most famous entities ever created is the Fotamecus egregore that Fenwick Rysen created. This entity is well known in chaos magic circles and used to manipulate time. The Fotamecus egregore focuses time into compression, with the idea being that this entity would change the flow of time so that a person working with this entity could manipulate time. The one aspect I never understood about Fotamecus was his fight with Chronos. Chronos in this case is perceived as: "...the god of fixed time, TIME; that which enslaves us, imprisons us in its rigidity, its chronic chronology" (Indifference Productions-Razor Smile #1). I figured that even with Fotamecus, a person is still acknowledging the hold Chronos has, because even with the manipulation of time, you can't escape it. You can make it run faster or slower, but you can't escape it, if you perceive such an opponent in the nature of time itself. So my thought on this part of the Fotamecus experience is that Fotamecus can actually work *with* Chronos, and accordingly on any occasion I've worked with this egregore I have done so with that understanding in mind. Fotamecus is an egregore because of the number of people who use him, so much so that he has become less dependent upon, and more fixed in, space/time as a being in his own right.

In *Creating Magickal Entities*, I discuss a space/time entity I created called Cerontis. Cerontis had a different goal from Fotamecus, and as far as I can tell never became an egregore, being instead a servitor and therefore reliant on the energy I choose to give him. His purpose for existence is as follows: "the entity makes me aware of possibilities I can use to improve myself, and to further my agenda in this world. The benefits of the entity are invaluable. Not only does it watch out for my potential interests, but also it makes me aware of those interests" (Creating Magical Entities – 2003, *Cunningham, Ellwood, & Wagener,* p. 113). Naturally, I end up making the choice as to whether or not I'll take advantage of the opportunity. But I do find that Cerontis works very effectively for me. Since I first created him, I have been made aware of countless opportunities, and needless to say, as is evidenced by this book you're holding in your hands right now, I've taken advantage of those opportunities. How Cerontis works is that he scans space/time for me for any probability that relates to my interests, and then notifies me of it, by synchronizing the probability with this reality. I encounter the probability and then I make a choice. Would I be as successful as I am in my life without Cerontis? I don't believe I would be. Having an entity that can navigate space/time looking for specific probabilities and then synchronizing those probabilities to my reality has made me aware of more opportunities than I would otherwise encounter. The entity has perspective and awareness that is focused on manipulating space/time for the express purpose of bringing probabilities to my attention. In our daily lives, it's so easy to get caught up in living, working, and otherwise dealing with everyday stresses that we tend to miss out on opportunities. By having Cerontis working on my behalf, I am made aware of probabilities that otherwise I might ignore because of the simple fact that I don't have the leisure to scan space/time for every opportunity I'd want to manifest. But creating an entity to do this for me has worked well.

Since my work with Cerontis, I've only created one other space/time entity. It's based on a board game called *Time*

Control. In the game, each person has time agents they send into the past to change the time line. I figured that the entity can draw energy to do its work from the concept of the game, as well as any time a person plays the game. And its work in this case is to help a magician with retroactive magical workings. Since the idea of the game is that a person goes back in time to change the past, I figured a retroactive magic entity can draw on that idea and aid a person in that pursuit. The name of the entity is Cimeral, which occurs as a result of the reduction of letters in the words "time control." Cimeral's purpose is to aid a person in working retroactive magic by adding energy to the retroactive act, and creating an impetus for change in the past that will ripple into the future. Cimeral can be drawn upon by simply evoking him when you do a retroactive magic working and asking him for aid in that working, with the understanding that he will add energy to the retroactive magic working, as well as help shift probabilities into existence for you so that the past is changed.

There are other kinds of entities you can create for space/time workings. It all depends on what you want to do with space/time magic. For more information on entity creation, please check out *Creating Magickal Entities*.

Appendix D
Space/Time Magic:

Several Pop Culture Approaches

It's fair to say that a lot of my ideas concerning space/time magick come from pop culture, and while my book, *Pop Culture Magick*, deals with some of those ideas, I've since had time to go into more depth with a couple of them. What I find most fascinating about the approaches to space/time magic are the theories that different Science Fiction or Fantasy authors come up with. I don't know if the authors practice magic or not, in some cases, so when the theories sound viable, or sound like they can work, I'm always intrigued by the authors.

The *Deathgate Cycle* is an excellent example of this. The first two books contain appendices that explain the magic systems and not in an *AD&D* style of explanation:

> Reality is simply the manifestation of intersecting waves of possibility. It is a vast and almost incomprehensible weave of solid physics in the midst of a myriad of infinite potentials. Science, technology, and biology all use the woven rope of reality. Magic, on the other hand, functions by reweaving the fabric of reality. A wizard begins by concentrating on the wave of probabilities rather than on reality itself. Through his learning and his powers, he looks out upon the myriad waves of infinite possibilities to find that part of the wave where his desired reality would be true. Then the wizard creates a harmonic wave of possibility to bend the existing wave so that what was once possible becomes part of what is true.
>
> (Dragon Wing – 1990, *Weis & Hickman,* p. 419)

While some of the terms come across a bit New Agey, the ideas presented here are not so far from how you can approach space/time magic. Certainly, I've integrated these concepts into my approach, finding that they do make sense, and corroborate how I do space/time magic. And what is really intriguing is that this approach goes beyond mere theory, as the practitioner in this fantasy series incorporates the use of runes (though it would be far more accurate to call what they use sigils). And the approach, in my opinion and from my practices with it, is useable for doing space/time magic, or, for that matter, other magical operations: "The key to rune (or runic) magic is that the harmonic wave that weaves a possibility into existence must be created with as much simultaneity as possible. This means that the various motions, signs, words, thoughts, and elements that go into making up the harmonic wave must be completed as close together as possible. The more simultaneous the harmonic wave structure, the more balance and harmony will be maintained in the wave and the more powerful the magic itself" (Dragon Wing – 1990, *Weis & Hickman,* p. 422). The reason that the language used to describe the possibility must be so close together is because the language is the magic. In fact, the language essentially operates as a non-linear referential system, where each part of the language is reliant upon the other to express the probability being manifested into reality. To some degree, we see this with English and other modern languages. Usually one word won't describe the situation.

The really cool aspect about the *Deathgate Cycle* is that it details two theories of magic, when it comes to the understanding and manipulation of reality. The second approach still incorporates the runes, but in a different manner, focusing on the power of the name: "In Patryn magic, an object's name defines precisely the state of the object relative to the underlying wave of possibility. Naming an object completely is critical to the level of success that the Patryn will have in later 'renaming' the object into an alternate state or form" (Elven Star 1991, *Weis & Hickman,* p. 362). The idea here in naming the object is for the practitioner to understand how that object relates to the wave of possibility. They then align that understanding with the altered state that would be induced by a new name for the object with which they work. Actually, what is occurring here is an employment of sympathetic magic, where the magician uses the dialectic between the runes to manipulate the wave of possibilities to manifest a specific possibility into reality. However, the magician has to be careful in that s/he needs to keep the name balanced with the object being named, or the magic becomes unbalanced, and consequently unravels. Ironically enough, this principle of naming has been used in magic before the series came out:

> The purpose behind the principle of naming anyone or anything at all, is to direct and hold the Energy of Consciousness in some particular way at some particular point or portion of Existence...After all, he [referring to the magician] is a focal point (or name) between the different states of the same Existence. Energies exchange each way through him. If those energies are balanced and beneficial through him, well and good, but if not, then chaos and disharmony will certainly cause some kind of damage or disadvantage.
> (Inner Traditions of Magic -1970, *William G. Gray*, p. 48)

In other words, the name serves not merely to describe, but also to stabilize the energy that defines the object or person, as well as explaining how that energy relates to the wave of probability. As the name is changed, so too is the nature of the reality of the object. Again, these ideas are useable for the magician, and are also related to how we use language. It truly becomes a matter of working with the concepts, more so than worrying about where they came from. In this case, pop culture offers a valuable way of understanding how the magic can work.

In the chapter on technology, I mentioned I would put together a space/time ritual that you could use with the mind machine that would also draw on pop culture. This ritual is based on my workings with the Deharan system of magic, and relates specifically to the magical work I've done with Aghama. For me, the Dehar Aghama represents a deity of space/time. The reason for this is because of how he is described in the *Wraeththu* trilogy, or more specifically, how his powers are described. Firstly, he's the progenitor of his race, and by the end of the trilogy he casts off his mortal flesh and goes to a different plane of existence. Also, even in his mortal flesh, he is able to put others into a state of timelessness, suspending space/time. Perhaps you can see why he appeals to me.

In any case, in this ritual I call on Aghama and have him take me on a journey, and be a guide through the DNA of the universe. The nice aspect about this ritual is that if you don't want to work with the Dehar you can just replace him with whatever you're comfortable with. Ultimately what's important is the efficacy of the ritual for you.

I like to start my rituals to the Dehara skyclad. I will also pull out body paints and paint on myself the symbols of the Dehar I will work with. If you're interested in this magic system, then check out *Grimoire Dehara (Storm Constantine, 2005)*, which will have the symbols in it. I work with four other Dehara in this ritual: Aruhani, Lunil, Miyacala, and Agave. These Dehara are used to help set up the sacred space in which you work. On my body, I paint their symbols around Aghama's symbol and my own. I also call upon the Dehara, vibrating: "Astale (name of Dehar)." This helps to create a connection between the entities I'm working with and me.

When I create my sacred space, I like to use my collection of stone eggs as physical markers of the space. You don't need to do this, but can use other artifacts that might have similar meaning for you. I find it useful for declaring my intention to create the space and charging that intention by the meaning I associate with the stones. What matters is that you do create a space. Make sure the dream or mind machine is with you in the circle, as it's an important part of the ritual.

Once I've called the four Dehara, I then call Aghama. The following is the chant I use to call him:

"Aghama, lord of space-time
Brightest star that shines above us and within us

182

Take us to the DNA of the Universe,
Open us to the secrets of space/time,
Of imagination that turns into reality,
Of reality that turns into imagination,
Open us to the essence of the universe,
To the manifestation of possibilities,
The awareness of all realms,
Take us to the web of power, Oh Aghama,
And through it help us to know ourselves,
Not merely as flesh and blood beings,
But also as beings of imagination and reality,
Of space and time,
Help us to balance ourselves,
Finding imagination and reality,
Together balanced, offering peace and love,
Imagination and will, let us find and know ourselves,
In all realities, in all imaginations, in space and time,
Show us the way to the web of power,
The DNA of the universe,
The imagination-reality-space-time all of us are."

You can use this chant or one of your own devising to call Aghama or whatever entity you work with to help you. Feel free to change the words as well. Generally, this kind of working is one where you're calling a guide. Occasionally when I do this working, I do it with either the dream or mind machine. I'll use the machine as a medium, a place where I first get in touch with the patterns of reality. The machine constructs a place of power through sound and light. In that place of power you can meet the entity of your choice and work with him/her/it. But you can also use meditation as well. Either meditation or the dream/mind machine works, and in some ways I prefer meditation, but I also like to incorporate technology into how I do magic. When I meditate or use the machines, I also like to use sex magic as the catalyst for the work. I find with my workings with the Dehara that sex magic is a powerful trigger for the actual experience. I'll usually pleasure myself right until the orgasm hits, and then ride the orgasm into a different state of mind. When combined with meditation or the machines, this tends to heighten the experience of your consciousness being altered. The reason this happens is because you are receiving a variety of stimuli on more than one level. Climaxing, when using the mind machine for instance, will really accelerate the patterns you perceive. The energy from the orgasm goes right into the altered state of mind you're experiencing and pushes it up a notch.

With an altered consciousness, I feel much more in touch with space/time and with the paradigms I use. When I originally did this ritual to Aghama, I also felt very connected to him and to what he showed me. He took me on a guided tour of sorts of the universe, and showed me how the energy that connects everything together works. Granted, this was my experience. And yours may be different, but what I experienced was the vibration of energy, the coalescing of patterns through how the energy of a person, place, event, etc. affected other people. I also came to understand how you could tug those connections, work with them to not only manifest events in your reality, but also even create connections between yourself and others. Admittedly, this is something we do every day, but how purposeful is our ability to connect with someone?

I close the ritual when I've concluded the meditation, usually just doing a standard thank you and dismissal of the forces I've worked with. I'm not being too technical with this description of the ritual. I want you to take the bones of it and add to it in whatever way you feels works for you. In the end, magical practice is ultimately a personal matter, and learning how to make someone's idea work for you is part of that process of creating your own system of magic.

Appendix E
Powerspots and Time Bubbles

In *Pop Culture Magick*, I mentioned my fascination with a TV series called *Yu Yu Hakusho*. In that series there were people who could alter the laws of reality in a limited space. The space was larger or smaller depending on the will power of the person involved. Also, the people had specific powers, for instance, being able to read a mind, or step on a person's shadow and keep them paralyzed. Also, although the characters could activate their space and use it to alter reality, their space could be destroyed if they were killed or knocked out of consciousness.

In space/time magic, we can manipulate the laws of reality around us. Those laws, after all, are really not set in stone. We only know of those laws because science has described them, but what scientists forget is that what they are describing is based on human experience, as opposed to some infallible agency. As such, the laws of reality are always suspect. For instance, consider that before Newton came up with the theories of gravity, gravity in and of itself did not exist. This might sound odd, but no one had conceptualized that gravity existed beforehand. No one had thought about why they would always fall back to the ground when they jumped up from it. Gravity as a law (which is another concept in and of itself) didn't come into existence until Newton first worded the concept. With that understanding in mind, I think it is possible to shape the laws of reality around us. I wouldn't be a magician if I didn't think so. I can't say we have absolute control of those laws, but we can work with them, shape them, and shape our understanding of reality as well.

I think what really intrigued me about the concept of territories (the limited space) in *Yu Yu Hakusho* was that the characters who had these territories were essentially living power spots. The power of the territory is determined by the nature of the character, and that also fascinated me. A power spot is a place of power. It contains a lot of power, which can be accessed by people. Usually a power spot is a place to which people are drawn. Raymire's Hollow in Pennsylvania is a power spot, albeit negatively charged due to certain events that have occurred in that space. Whipp's Ledges, in North Eastern Ohio, is another example. Power spots resonate with energy, and usually this energy also embodies the nature of the land. In the case of Raymire's Hollow, the energy is negative because of the murder of Raymire by a fellow wizard. That death tainted the energy of the land, which was used by Raymire to power his spells.

Cities also have power spots. These spots are not as obvious as the natural parks we can go to, but nonetheless they can be found. It's just a matter of attuning yourself to the flow of the energy, specifically where it's going physically. Once you can feel that direction of energy, follow it and eventually you'll find your power spot.

It is possible to create power spots of your own. For instance, I created one at Kent State University, the first year I attended school there. I noticed, when I first arrived, the amount of sun imagery that was not only displayed by the school but also the locals. I decided to do a solar working, in which I would use the sun's energy as part of the process of creating and attuning the power spot to me. What I ended up doing was walking around Kent State at night, placing spit sigils on the ground and other spots that really resonated with me. The idea was that when the sun rose, the energy of it would hit the energy of the spit sigils, and impress that energy into the land. In this way, I was not only able to create a power spot, but also attune it to my energy. I do find it essential to wander around, as this allows you to find the power spots: "If you wander with the sole purpose of following signs of power, you will more often than not obtain significant results. Even if, at the beginning, we find only small powers, yet with that small power we may prepare ourselves for greater power, and so on until we find all we need" (Addressing Power – 1996, *Stephen Mace*, p. 83). The wandering allows you to know the character of the land, and in turn allows the land to know your character. This is important, because you aren't just finding a power spot. You're also establishing a relationship between yourself and the place from which you're tapping the power. It's best to have a good relationship, and sometimes you have to make efforts to show your earnestness before the power of a place will work with you. For instance, I ended up walking in a homecoming parade for Kent State, something I'd never normally do, but I knew it would show the entity of Kent State my interest in working with it.

And with mention of entity comes the second aspect of the power spot. You won't just work with power when you find such a spot. You'll work with the entity of that spot, the spirit of the land, place, or event that you've come across. Mace brings up an interesting aspect of his work with the spirit of a tavern:

> Nor need you have any concern over exploiting the elemental, since giving its human occupants a boost is as much to its advantage as the humans'. After all, if the elemental of a tavern helps a band be brilliant, it'll help pack in the customers, pay the mortgage, and keep the place from being torn down to build a shopping mall. It's a symbiotic relationship, no sort of parasitism at all.
> (Addressing Power – 1996, *Stephen Mace*, p. 88)

When you work with a power spot, you enter into a symbiotic relationship with it. For example, when I first began working with the elemental spirits, and particularly with the power spots where I lived, I gave blood as an offering and an exchange of essence. In this way, the spirit of the land was not just giving of itself, but was also receiving. The thing to remember is that any place can be a power spot, though not all places will be good ones. I like to make the buildings in which I live into power spots. I deal with the energy of the building, which is an entity, and create a symbiotic relationship between it and myself. If you do anything like this, remember to do so with good energy. You should not attempt to bond with a place where the energy off-sets you. It'll just bring you trouble.

How these physical power spots relate to the concept of territories is that like the territories, power spots tend to be places that warp reality just a bit. And although any place can be made into a power spot, obviously not all places are power spots to start with. I remember, from my time of working with Raymire's Hollow, that the reality of that place was always different from the area around it. For one thing, no matter the time of day, the place was always dark. And, at night, people tended to see spirits and other phenomena there. Perhaps they expected to see spirits, and so they did, but even if that was the case, then the power at that place picked up on those expectations and made them reality.

If you become bonded to a power spot, it is possible to work with the reality in that area. I decided, shortly after being introduced to the concept of territories in the aforementioned TV show, that I would try to create a different law of reality than what normally existed. The winters can be very cold and bitter in Northeastern Ohio, and in the winter of 2004 I didn't have a car, so to get groceries I often had to walk, because the bus line didn't go to where I lived. I created a rule that whenever it was cold, the energy of the power spot, which was linked to me, would flow through me and cause me to be warm. The first time I did this, I felt as if my body became a living generator. The energy came through me so fast that I had to envision generators that could process that energy. I was certainly warm, but I was also channeling a lot of energy through me and as such was exhausted once I'd come home from the walk. I also had the smell of ozone around me, due to the process of heating that was being worked through my body. After that experience, I knew I needed to be careful with how I shaped the law of reality, as I could have burned myself out. However, consequent experiences of heating myself by establishing a law of reality were mixed. Sometimes it worked and sometimes it didn't. As time goes on, I hope to continue to refine this process, but I can safely say it will probably take some time. No technique I've either learned or developed happens over night. Trial and error is essential to good experimentation.

I now incorporate two other experiments into the process. I'll usually hum a song I really like when I'm visualizing a space with altered rules of reality. The humming of the song becomes the vibration that empowers that space and enables the altered rule of reality to take place. Certainly when I have not hummed, the experiment has not worked. Another experiment Maryam and I have done during the winter is to draw heat from passing cars to warm ourselves. Heat is a byproduct of the car, but it is also useful, and can be used to keep you warm. Simply visualize the heat coming from the car and wrap it around yourself. This second experiment, while not altering the rule of a given area of space, has shown me how you can take resources in your environment around you and use them for magic.

Another way I have experimented with determining laws of reality in a given space is with the concept of the time bubble. This is a concept I think we all use at one time or another. A fellow magician, who was on the timemachines e-list I ran before writing this book, coined the name itself. In any case, I'm sure that some of you can remember a time when you were running late for a meeting or for a bus and you thought, "If only there was a way to slow down time." Then you found to your surprise you made the meeting on time or you made it to the bus stop a couple minutes before the driver showed up. What you may not have realized is that you actually slowed time around you and sped up time for yourself.

How does this work? Much like the concept of a territory, the time bubble is a space of energy, usually, in fact, your personal space. This space reacts to your subconscious signals all the time and not just in relationship to time. The time bubble works with the understanding that you speed up your perception of time, causing you to move faster. While this occurs, the flow of time external to your bubble slows down, or seems to. Really what's happening is that you cause yourself to move through time faster than you normally would, projecting yourself into the future with a specific result in mind. Time hasn't really slowed down, but you have sped up, and to your perception it seems slower as a result. After doing this technique I always find that my metabolism has sped up as well. But I also find myself making it on time to the bus stop so I can catch my ride to wherever I'm going. What I, and apparently others, visualize is a bubble of time around me. This bubble moves time faster for the person inside it. I tend to visualize my bubble as a transparent aquamarine color.

I've also experimented with territories by blending my energy into that of the territory/power spot. Since I'm symbiotically attached to it, this is very easy to do, and is similar to Burrough's invisibility technique. The difference really is that you're not going around looking at people first so you can be invisible to them (and consequently limiting their awareness of you), which is what Burrough's technique is. Rather I envision myself as a chameleon. My energy signature becomes the energy signature of the land I'm working with. I become indistinguishable from the land. I've found this to be rather useful in not only being invisible to other magicians, but also in building up the sympathetic relationship between myself and my power spot. This technique also makes it very easy to draw on the energy of the power spot, as in a sense you've become part of it.

I have also worked with power spots by attaching myself to the energy of the Earth and then extending from the Earth to the other planets and stars, creating leylines between those heavenly bodies and myself. The purpose of that is quite simply to draw upon the power within the planets and stars, as well as furthering my understanding of the concepts involved in working with them for space/time magic.

There is also the matter of applying different paradigms of magic to the power spots we work with. For instance, a person who can use Reiki or other healing "energies" could attune a particular place to those energies and use that place as a way of enhancing his or her own healing, as well as healing the land around him/her. Also, I like to use sigils when I attune a power spot to my energy. The sigil represents the symbiosis I seek between myself and the spirit of the power I'm working with. One intriguing aspect about power spots is that they can tap you into the energy of others who have worked with them, or even simply worked in the area. The power spot is a recorder of all the magical workings that have been done there and you can not only access that recorder, but also retroactively join in with those workings by simply being attuned to the power of a place. Of course, you should use discretion if you choose to do this, as the people who worked magic in the area before you might not have wanted someone to tamper with what they did. Be wary, but don't hesitate to experiment, experience, and explore what others have done as a way of understanding space/time magic.

There is still a lot of rough territory with this kind of space/time magic. I've only been experimenting with the idea of altering "rules" of reality for the last year and a half. And while any of us could argue that we already do that anyway, there's something to be said for tapping into the physical locality around you and shaping the reality of that locality. But you'll need to put in time, effort, and experimentation to yield further results. I've given you some idea of what I've been working with, and as time goes on I hope to keep people updated, so that this area of space/time magic becomes more refined. The reason I've included this appendix is because I do feel it's important to show a work in progress instead of just the finished technique. I never stop working with or improving on my techniques for magical practice, because there's always room to improve. Hopefully I have inspired you toward that approach as well.

Appendix F
Space/Time Magic:

Time Management

One skill I have is the ability to manage my time effectively. Between teaching two classes, attending classes full time at a grad school, writing fulltime, and traveling to promote my writing, I don't actually get a lot of free time. So I have to make the most of it, and that's not always as easy as it sounds. I think of time management as a form of space/time magic. It takes a truly talented person to balance everything in his/her life and have time to relax. Yet every semester, my school work is done a full two to three weeks before the semester is over. I see many stressed out grad students around me, but each night I get a full night's sleep.

I do this by managing my time, by knowing exactly how and when to work on a paper or an article. I never overextend myself with promises to other people or other commitments. I will do what I can, when I can, but my pleasure comes before anything else. This is an important priority, and one that is neglected by many people around me. People work themselves to death each day, and go home and sleep for a few hours and start up again. Is that the kind of life you want to live? I know it isn't for me.

The way I work time management in terms of magic is to perceive the task at hand as one that can be accomplished over time, as opposed to frantically rushing to complete it. I'll spend a couple of hours a night typing a paper, and then go and relax. Time does not dictate our existence; we dictate *its* existence. Likewise, we must do the same with events that occur in our lives. Discipline yourself to work incrementally, as opposed to all at once. Believe it or not, it takes more discipline to do work in increments than it does to write a paper in a night. The incremental work demands that you spend time each day putting effort into the task. But the payoff is that the task doesn't take as much mental effort to finish, and you have time to relax and enjoy living life. The discipline will also help you in your magical practices, because it will show you how to focus, and also when to know when to stop so that you can achieve better focus the next time. By learning to manage time, to balance the work in increments, you can live life more fully.

The magic, in the end, is not some symbol or a flourish of a wand. It is the disciplining of your mind, the focus on the moment at hand, and the realization that any moment is just that, a moment. You can make a moment as long as you want, but you should also know when to let the moment go and experience another one. So to manage your time, do not let the task dictate how you deal with it. Deal with it in increments; stretch the moment out, so it becomes a pocket of time that you can reenter whenever you need it, but does not define the circumstance you are in. The only aspect that should define any circumstance is you. At the very least, you can control how you react, and take advantage of the situation, and time management is part of that.

Appendix G
Day Dreaming the Future

In Konton 2.1, Brian Shaughnessy suggested that memories could be manufactured and made into reality through the use of nostalgia:

> Our idea of whom we are is based on memories of our experiences, memories that often deviate from the actuality of the events in question. People who live in the past dwell on nostalgic memories, not on the minutia of the past...If we can teach ourselves to forge a bond between that feeling of nostalgia, and a manufactured memory, we will be able to cause the brain to transcribe the short term experience of a manufactured memory, we will be able to cause the brain to transcribe the short term experience of a manufactured event into a memory as long-lived, and powerful as the memory of our first love.
> (Manufacturing Memories - 2005, *Brian Shaughnessy,* p. 17)

Through creative visualization and a bonding to an energy such as nostalgia, it is very possible to manufacture memories and perform retroactive magic, making those memories into reality. However, one question that occurs, is that if we can do this with the past, why can't we do it with the future? One of the puzzling conundrums that faces modern physicists when it comes to the human memory is the inability of mind to have "memories" of the future, in the same way that we have "memories" of the past. And yet even our memories of the past are suspect, as Shaughnessy points out above. I suspect, however, that we actually do have "memories" of the future, but the mechanism by which we receive these "memories" is perceived as a form of dreaming – day dreaming, to be exact.

Everyday, if even for a moment, the mind drifts away from the tasks around it and dreams, and in that dreaming the person perceives the shaping of the future, the possible memories from the future being handed back to him/her by a future self, or by the desire to escape the present monotony in his/her life. A particularly vivid form of this day dreaming is déjà vu, which can be very similar to a lucid dream, in terms of how real the scene feels. Although many people perceive déjà vu to be a remembrance of the past, this is an incorrect assumption on their part. Usually when someone has déjà vu, they vividly experience a future probable memory *before* it occurs. When you actually experience that moment, you will realize it is déjà vu, but will likely not realize that you can change that actual moment.

We trick ourselves into believing that déjà vu is a past memory, even as we trick ourselves into believing that day dreams are just idle fantasies. But we can't be sure that the day dreams and déjà vu aren't flashes from the future. For me, the déjà vu has always pointed to a future event. I believe the vividness of the déjà vu experience is a bleed over effect, the future possibility seeping into the present reality. The key to understanding this is realizing that when you experience a vivid moment and feel as if you're living it again, it's likely déjà vu, and you're likely experiencing a possible future.

The first experience of déjà vu will play itself out, and chances are you'll feel like you're watching a film. But when the actual future possibility manifests, and you are experiencing that moment in your present, then you can manipulate the possibility into a different reality. As an example, I had a deja vu experience where one of my girl friends was a playing a game, and I made a comment that made her very angry. When the actual experience occurred, and I recognized what was happening, I avoided making the comment, and altered the future probability.

The frustrating aspect about déjà vu is that it's random. As far as I can tell there's no guarantee when you'll experience and what you'll experience. And it can be years before you actually experience the déjà vu moment in reality. And it usually takes a few moments to recognize the actual experience of déjà vu. Déjà vu is practically useless for the purposes of a magician, unless déjà vu experiences can be induced. That can occur through meditation, but in the end, working with day dreams is a much better way of manifesting possible future "memories."

Day dreams are less concrete than déjà vu, but they occur more frequently, and are easy to mold. The day dream usually represents a future possibility: a place you'd like to be, something you'd like to be doing. Most people don't think anything further about day dreams. A moment's fancy and then back to mundane reality. But for you, the day dream can become reality.

Just as memories are manufactured through nostalgia, so are day dreams manufactured by longing. The longing you feel to achieve a goal, or to be with someone, is just as potent as nostalgia. That longing can be used to shape your day dreams into potent visions of what could be. And those visions can be manifested into reality.

There are several ways to go about manifesting your day dreams into reality. One method I use is my variation of Shaughnessy's tesser-act technique, which I described in Chapter 9. This variation involves taking the two dimensional image of the tesser-act found in *Konton* issue 1 on page 46, and painting it on a ouija board, which is already a natural gateway for working with space/time. The tesser-act amplifies the ouija board's power, and at the same time acts as a containment field. For the purpose of the day dream magic, the tesser-act board serves as a wonderful tool for scrying and pathworking.

I always place the planchette in the middle of the board, in the middle of the tesser-act configuration. I place fingers from both of my hands on it, close my eyes, and direct my energy into the planchette. Usually what I'll do is visualize the day dream, just let my thoughts drift toward a future I'd like to manifest. I'll focus on specific details, try to make the dream as specific as possible with everything that occurs. The goal is to manifest those details into reality, and the dream allows you to explore those details to your heart's content. Even if the details seem impossible, day dream it anyway…it's a day dream, but it can become reality. Once you've dreamed to your satisfaction, visualize the dream moving from the scrying planchette into your hands. Take your hands off the board and project the energy into reality, visualizing the day dream merging into reality. I usually see a ripple in the air around me when I do this. Bear in mind that you want the day dream to manifest in the near future, so you're evoking a possibility that will manifest in a couple of days/weeks/months.

The second method I use is through meditation. In June of 2005, my car had several problems that the mechanic had been unable to diagnose, because finding information on my car was hard, as my car is a limited edition. I laid down in a corpse pose and did pranayamic breathing until I began to meditate, and then focused on day dreaming about the car and the mechanic. I saw the mechanic getting the appropriate information, and then fixing all the problems in my car. When I came out of the meditation, I again focused on the energy in my hands, and projected it into reality, visualizing the day dream merging into this reality. The mechanic did end up finding a wiring diagram for my car, and was able to fix the problems so that they no longer occurred. There's no real difference between using the tesser-act board or the meditation, so use whichever technique is easier for you to manifest your day dreams into reality.

The key to working with your day dreams is longing. How much do you really want this dream to come into reality? What are you willing to do to achieve this dream? The emotion of long is an emotion that calls for better circumstances, for better situations that you feel you deserve to have in your life. While many people dream of those situations, you can take your dreams and your longings, and push them into reality. When you do day dream, feel the longing, identify what it is you long for. Even a simple longing to escape from the tedium of your job is a powerful energy, and may indicate that you need to change that job. Use your longing to show you where you might want to be, where you feel your talents would be useful for you, and then use that day dream to motivate you to action. Focus in the dream on finding job listings for your ideal job, filling out applications, and sending resumes in. Then push that dream into reality, and most importantly, take action. You can do magic to shift your situation, but you still have to do some of the physical gruntwork. Whatever you day dream for, though, realize that your longing can make it reality, no matter how impossible it may seem. We tell ourselves something is impossible, and believe it because we've been taught to think that way. But the truth is quite the opposite: nothing is so far out of our reach that we can't manifest it into our lives.

On a final note, remember that even as you do this dream work, it may take time for that day dream to become reality. Keep your mind open to opportunities, and don't worry about the day dream. Let it shift its way into reality. Your longing is a beacon to the day dream, and will manifest it into reality, aided by the actions you take to pursue your goal. Everyday you drift into a dream, a potential reality that could be. Would you rather that dream wasted away, showing you better circumstances, but leaving you filled with an empty, unfulfilled longing? Or would you rather take your dream and manifest into reality, seeking and achieving what you desire? I know my choice. What's yours?

Bibliography

Brennan, J. H. (2002). Occult Tibet: Secret practices of Himalayan magic. St. Paul: Llewellyn Publications.

Burroughs, William S. (1985). The adding machine: Selected essays. New York: Arcade Publishing.

Carroll, Peter. (1992). Liber kaos. York Beach: Samuel Weiser, Inc.

Carroll, Peter. (1995). Pysber magick: Advanced ideas in chaos magick. Tempe, New Falcon Publications.

Carroll, Peter. (2002). Cutting edge theory. Chaos International, 25. 26-29.

Cunningham, David Michael, Ellwood, Taylor, & Wagener, *Amanda R.. (2003).* Creating magickal entities. Perrysburg: Egregore Publishing.

David-Neel, Alexandra. (1971). Magic and mystery in Tibet. New York: Dover Publications, Inc.

David-Neel, Alexandra. (1988). Bandits, priests, and demons. The Hague: Uitgeverij Sirius en Siderius.

Drury, Neville. (2003). Austin Osman Spare: Divine draughtsman. In Richard Metzger (ed.) Book of lies: The disinformation guide to magick and the occult. New York: The Disinformation Company Ltd.

Gray, William G. (1969). Magical ritual methods. York Beach: Samuel Weiser, Inc.

Gray, William G. (1970). Inner traditions of magic. York Beach: Samuel Weiser, Inc.

Greene, Brian. (1999). The elegant universe: Superstrings, hidden dimensions, and the quest for the ultimate theory. New York: W.W. Norton & Company.

Greer, Mary K. (1988). Tarot mirrors: Reflections of personal meaning. North Hollywood: New Castle Publishing Co., Inc.

Hawking, Stephen. (2001). The universe in a nutshell. New York: Bantam Books.

Hebdige, Dick. (1971). Subculture: The meaning of style. New York: Routledge, Taylor, & Francis.

Hine, Phil. (1993). Prime Chaos: Adventures in Chaos Magick. Tempe: New Falcon Publications.

Hine, Phil. (1995). Condensed chaos: An introduction to chaos magic. Tempe: New Falcon Books.

Hoey, Michael. (1994). Signalling in discourse: A functional analysis of a common discourse pattern in written and spoken English. In Malcolm Coulthard (Ed.) Advances in written text analysis. New York: Routledge, Taylor, & Francis Group. 26-45.

Indifference Productions. (2002). Fotemacus. Razor Smile, 1. Brighton: No page numbers listed.

Knight, Gareth. (1996). The Magical World of Tarot: Fourfold Mirror of the Universe. York Beach: Samuel Weiser, Inc.

Konstantinos. (1995). Summoning spirits: The art of magical evocation. St. Paul: Llewellyn Publications.

Mace, Stephen. (1984). Stealing the fire from heaven. Milford: Self-published.

Mace, Stephen. (1993). Squeezing being: A modern approach to reality manipulation. Milford: Self-published.

Mace, Stephen. (1996). Addressing power: Sixteen essays on magick and the politics it implies. Milford: Self-published.

Mace, Stephen. (1999). Sorcery as virtual mechanics. Portland: Dagon Productions.

McCloud, Scott. (1993). Understanding Comics: The Invisible Art. New York: Paradox Press.

Moore, Alan. (1986-1987). Watchmen. New York: DC Comics.

Morrison, Grant (2003). Pop magic! In Richard Metzger (ed.) <u>Book of lies: The disinformation guide to magick and the occult</u>. New York: The Disinformation Company Ltd. 16-25.

Odier, Daniel. (1969). <u>The Job: Interviews with William S. Burroughs</u>. New York: Penguin Books.

Penczak, Christopher. (2001). <u>City magick: Urban rituals, spells and shamanism</u>. York Beach: Weiser Books.

Pirsig, Robert M. (1974). <u>Zen and the art of motorcycle maintenance</u>. New York: Bantam Books.

P-orridge, Genesis. (1996). Thee splinter test. In Christopher S. Hyatt Ed.) <u>Rebels & devils: The psychology of liberation</u>. Tempe: New Falcon Publications. 335-362.

P-orridge, Genesis. (2003). Magick squares and future beats: The magical process and methods of William S. Burroughs and Brion Gysin. (Richard Metzger (ed.) <u>Book of lies: The disinformation guide to magick and the occult</u>. New York: The Disinformation Company Ltd. 103-117.

P-orridge, Genesis. (2003). Virtual mirrors in solid time: The prophetic portals of Austin Osman Spare. In Richard Metzger (ed.) <u>Book of lies: The disinformation guide to magick and the occult</u>. New York: The Disinformation Company Ltd. 127-137.

Renee, Janic (1990). <u>Tarot spells</u>. St. Paul: Llewellyn Publications.

Roberts, Jane. (1974). <u>The Nature of Personal Reality</u>. New York: Bantam Books.

Ross, Kenneth A., & Wright, Charles R. B. (1999). <u>Discrete mathematics, fourth edition</u>. Upper Saddle River: Prentice Hall.

Shaughnessy, Brian. (2004). Tesseract magick. <u>Konton, 1</u>. 45-47.

Shaughnessy, Brian. (2005). Manufacturing memories. <u>Konton, 2.1</u>. 17-20.

Talbot, Michael. (1991). <u>The holographic universe</u>. New York: HarperCollins Publishers Inc.

The Anti-Group Collective. <u>Psychophysicist</u>. Liner notes.

The Anti-Group Collective. <u>Meontological Research Recordings Teste Tones</u>. Liner notes.

Townley, Kevin. (2003). <u>Meditations on the cube of space</u>. Santa Maria: Archer Books.

Turner, Greg. (2004). Acoustic sigils. <u>Razor smile, 2</u>. Brighton. 37-45.

Wanless, James. (1998). <u>Voyager Tarot: Guidebook for the Journey</u>. Carmel: Merrill-West Publishing.

Weis, Margaret & Hickman, Tracy. (1990). <u>Dragon Wing</u>. New York: Bantam Books.

Weis, Margaret & Hickman, Tracy. (1991). <u>Elven Star</u>. New York: Bantam Books.

Wenger, Etienne. (1998). <u>Community of practice: Learning, meaning and identity</u>. Cambridge: Cambridge University Press.

Wilson, Robert Anton. (1990). <u>Quantum psychology: How brain software programs you and your world</u>. Tempe: New Falcon Publications

LaVergne, TN USA
31 January 2010
171648LV00002B/13/A